HOUSE

AND

SENATE

HOUSE
AND
SENATE

Ross K. Baker

W · W · Norton & Company

New York · London

FIRST EDITION

The text of this book is composed in Times Roman with display type set in Typositor Trump Gravur and Trump Mediaeval. Composition and manufacturing by the Haddon Craftsmen. Book design by Marjorie J. Flock.

Library of Congress Cataloging-in-Publication Data
Baker, Ross K.
  House and Senate / by Ross K. Baker.—1st ed.
    p.   cm.
  Includes index.
  1. United States.   Congress.   I. Title.
JK1061.B33 1989
328.73—dc19   89–3194
                                         CIP

ISBN 0-393-02706-6

W. W. Norton & Company, Inc., 500 Fifth Avenue, New York, N.Y. 10110
W. W. Norton & Company Ltd., 37 Great Russell Street, London WC1B 3NU

1 2 3 4 5 6 7 8 9 0

To my mother and father,
Augusta L. Baker and Maurice Baker,
wonderful parents and good friends.

Contents

Introduction

A SUSTAINED COMPARISON of the House and Senate is something that most people assume to exist. They are usually surprised to find that such a book is not to be found. Tantalizing parts of the drama have been written and there are even some summaries of House-Senate differences that are prized for their compactness.[1] I wanted to cover the difference in greater scope.

I realized that a book based on documentary sources alone might not provide enough richness of texture and detail to do justice to a relationship so multifaceted and subtle. I also was not certain that the House-Senate distinctions set forth in the literature constituted a complete inventory of differences. These concerns prompted me to interview people who could add to that category of differences or elaborate on those already recognized.

I conducted roughly sixty interviews in 1986 and 1987 with four groups of people: incumbent senators and former senators who had been first elected to the House; journalists whose beats include the two houses; lobbyists who visit both senators and House members; and staff who have served in both chambers.

The senators I spoke with ranged in age from eighty-year-old Hugh D. Scott, a Pennsylvania Republican whose service began in the House before Pearl Harbor and ended in the Senate as minority leader in 1977, to forty-four-year-old Christopher Dodd, a Connecticut Democrat who was sworn in as a House freshman in December 1974. Among the past and present senators I interviewed were a former presidential candidate (George S. McGovern, the Democratic standard-bearer in 1972); Ro-

nald Reagan's first choice for a running mate (Senator Richard
S. Schweiker of Pennsylvania, chosen by Reagan in his unsuccessful effort to head off the nomination of Gerald R. Ford in
1976); and the man who was closest of all his Senate colleagues
to John F. Kennedy, former senator George A. Smathers, a
Florida Democrat.

Among the journalists I interviewed are people whose
names are familiar to the daily newspaper reader or viewer of
television news. They include Steven Roberts of the *New York
Times;* Ann Compton of ABC-TV; Thomas Edsall of the
Washington Post; and Linda Wertheimer of National Public
Radio. Although the names of lobbyists are not, with a few
exceptions, household words, Washington insiders will recognize names such as Thomas A. Dine, director of the American-
Israel Public Affairs Committee; Bertram Carp, vice-president
of Turner Broadcasting; Howard Paster of Timmons and Company; and Jay Berman, president of the Recording Industry
Association.

Interviewing "elites," as these people are described by social
scientists, entails a set of challenges different from those en-
countered during mass surveys of public opinion with thousands of anonymous respondents or even from in-depth surveys
of ordinary citizens. Surveys are more structured and proceed
according to a set of questions that look to a certain uniformity
of response. Elite interviews are less manageable. Elite inter-
viewees are often skilled, through years of practice, at sidestep-
ping questions or even rephrasing questions to enable them to
provide the answer they want to give you. Some of the interviews were invaluable; others were of limited use. In the aggregate, however, they paint a picture of two houses of Congress
that have not merged into a single undifferentiated entity called
"Congress."

Sometimes the differences between the House and the Senate are so obvious and overwhelming that the logic the framers
of the Constitution expressed in a two-house national legislature is manifested with startling clarity; other differences are

expressed with such fineness and subtlety that only the *cognoscenti* can savor them. From time to time an incident occurs that reminds people, in a dazzling symbolic fashion, just how different the two houses are from each other.

One of these epiphanies occurred in the spring of 1986 at a time when Americans had been the targets of repeated acts of terrorism on foreign soil. Concern was expressed that outrages would soon be taking place in this country. Security was beefed up at the White House and at a number of federal facilities around the country. Then, in accordance with what Senator Daniel Patrick Moynihan calls "the iron law of emulation," the legislative branch of the United States government began to demand the same security measures that the executive branch was enjoying.

Significantly, however, the cry for tighter security around the U.S. Capitol was expressed with much greater urgency and passion in the Senate than in the House. While some senators condemned the proposal by a joint committee of House and Senate leaders to install a wrought-iron fence around the Capitol building, the initiative and the loudest defense of the fence came from the Senate.

Senator Alan K. Simpson of Wyoming, a man known for his levelheadedness and folksy, approachable manner, spearheaded the drive for the fence arguing that if a bomb like the one planted near the empty Senate chamber in November 1983 were to go off while the body was in session a dozen or more members might be killed. Simpson's Democratic counterpart, Minority Whip Alan Cranston of California, tried somewhat unconvincingly to make the project a little less self-serving by asserting that "we have a duty to do all we can" to protect tourists visiting the Capitol.[2]

The reaction of House members was more relaxed. Democratic representative Leon E. Panetta of California explained the opposition of many House members to the fence in terms of differences in the institutional personalities of both houses. "The atmosphere of the House is much different from the Senate," Panetta observed. "We have much more of a free flow here. There's much more mingling here between members and constituents." Former House Speaker Thomas P. O'Neill expressed skepticism about the fence, saying, "I'm not enthusiastic about it, to be perfectly truthful. This is the Capitol of the country, where laws are enacted every day. It ought to be a free institution."[3]

What came out of the episode was a sense that somehow the Senate was more worthy of protection than the House, but also that the House is simply closer to people than is the Senate and that the constitutional design that ordained this closeness has much vitality today.

The sense that somehow the senator is a special and distinct individual who stands above the *hoi polloi* more majestically than the House member comes through in very small ways that the newspapers rarely report. There is, for example, the matter of lapel pins.

At the beginning of every new Congress, members of the House are issued lapel pins. The designs of these pins change from Congress to Congress; some have featured the dome of the Capitol, others the ceremonial mace used to open the House, still others the Great Seal of the United States.

The purpose of these pins is to identify members of the House to the various congressional employees, most notably the Capitol Policemen who control traffic at the corner of Independence and New Jersey avenues and at the other aboveground crossings between the House office buildings, where members work, and the House chamber in the Capitol, where they vote. The pins are signals to hold up traffic so members can get inside the Capitol and vote or have access to places where the public is not admitted.

When I asked a U.S. senator if such distinctive pins were issued to new senators he reacted as if I had asked him whether they wore dunce caps or beanies. "Certainly not," he huffed.

Riding the subway car that runs through the connecting

corridors of the Senate office buildings in the period after the 1988 elections, one could see above the driver's control panel the photos of the ten newly elected senators. The pictures were posted so that the operator would know at a glance then for whom the cars would need to be held and to permit him to greet them by name. While there is a photographic directory of the 435 House members that is issued to all House offices, only a handful of people can recognize all House members by sight.

It is size, more than any other factor, that distinguishes the House from the Senate; the specific differences that flow from the fact that one body of the national legislature is more than four times larger than the other would alone mark these as two remarkably distinct institutions even if nothing else set them apart.

There are, of course, major distinctions of a constitutional nature that are important: the six-year senatorial term versus the two-year term for House members; the fact that senators represent entire states but House members—with the exception of the at-large members from Alaska, Delaware, Wyoming, North and South Dakota, and Vermont—represent districts within states consisting of roughly 550,000 people; and differences in legislative authority prescribed in Article I of the Constitution.

This book will make the point that the size difference is a most significant one. But I will illustrate the considerable advantages that redound to a smaller legislative body in an age in which national politics is so profoundly influenced by mass media that favor distinct personalities over large institutions.

To assert that important differences exist between the House and Senate is not a self-evident proposition. A respectable, indeed eminent, body of scholarly and official opinion holds that the differences between the House and the Senate have narrowed significantly. There is much to commend this "convergence theory," not the least of which is that many people believe it.[4]

No one would argue that the two houses are as distinct from each other, and in the same way, as they were in 1789. The ratification of the Seventeenth Amendment in 1913 made senators subject to popular election rather than election by the state legislatures, and this greatly narrowed the distance between the senators and the voters. The once-hierarchical House now resembles somewhat more closely the Senate where there are few gradations of power. The House has, on occasion, shown itself to be an estimable forum for debate on national issues, superseding a Senate once considered the preeminent forum for debating the great issues. Some House members have broken free of the rigid division of labor that forced them to restrict their pronouncements to the subject matter within the jurisdiction of their principal committee assignments. Even the difference in length of term looks less imposing as House incumbents have shown themselves almost invulnerable to challenges.

While acknowledging this evidence of convergence, or even reversal or rearrangement of some traditional characteristics, this book seeks to persuade the reader that important House-Senate differences persist. I will try to make the case by pointing out that members of both chambers know it. Journalists who cover Congress know it. People who lobby Congress know it. Staff members who have worked on both sides of the Capitol know it. Members of Congress, above all, know it.

Not only are the houses different, they are also distant, mutually suspicious, and inordinately prideful and sensitive.

Christopher Matthews, former press secretary and administrative assistant to former Speaker of the House O'Neill, provided his impression of working in a building shared by the House and Senate.

There's kind of an invisible shield across the rotunda. Senators can be on Capitol Hill for years and never cross the Capitol except to hear a State of the Union Message.

There's no reason why somebody over there would disgrace himself by going over to the House side, and the House member, for fear of humiliation, would never risk going over there.

Matthews's comments suggest something more than inno-
cent obliviousness of one house for another. Do they contain a
hint of rancor and resentment? I think that the ensuing chapters
will show that they do.

William S. White, the journalist who wrote on both the
Senate and House in the 1950s, captured a feeling prevalent
among House members in an anecdote about House Speaker
Sam Rayburn, who served for almost twenty years in that post.
Speaking to White about former House member Lyndon B.
Johnson, who went on to become the most powerful leader of
the Senate in modern times before being elected president, Ray-
burn said of his fellow Texan's shift to the Senate, "You know,
Bill, it was a sad thing—no it was a terrible thing—when old
Lyndon decided to leave here and go over yonder. If he had
stayed on here he could have been quite a powerful figure—in
a few more years."[5]

You get it from the other side as well. Former U.S. senator
Joseph Sill Clark, a Pennsylvania Democrat and an aristocrat
from Chestnut Hill, was asked some years ago if there existed
in the Senate the kind of informal "sociolegislative" lunch
groups and clubs that were so popular in the House. These
groups have names like "Acorns" and "SOS" and combine
serious discussion with good fellowship. Clark reacted with
shock and disdain. "Oh, God, no! The other body was scorned.
We'd never cavort like that."

Characteristically, Clark resorted to a euphemism—"the
other body"—to refer to the House. The word "Senate" was
actually ineffable in the House until a rules change took effect
on January 6, 1987, that allowed House members to call the
Senate by its proper name, rather than "the other body." Senators often use the more cumbersome phrase in a derisive manner.

If these incidents suggest that the two houses have nothing
to do with each other unless compelled to do so by the constitutional requirement that no bill shall become law unless passed
in identical form by both houses—a requirement necessitating

House-Senate conference committees that force the two chambers to interact—it might overstate the case, but not by much. In the course of the research for this book, I was shocked at how little contact there is between the House and Senate under normal circumstances.

A Sketch of Contemporary Bicameralism

Any discussion of the current state of the differences and similarities between the House and Senate must begin with a look at the formal basis of bicameralism—the use of a two-house legislature to make laws—found in the Constitution and early congressional practice. The first chapter, "Two Sides of the Capitol," contains a brief description of the intercameral relations over the past two centuries and of the changes in the status and prestige of the two chambers over the years. In this chapter I also discuss both the shared and distinctive legislative powers of the House and Senate.

The second and third chapters deal with those features and factors that seem, in the aggregate, to contribute most to House-Senate differences: those that arise from the stark differences in the sizes of the House and Senate. In Chapter 2 I discuss the relative importance of the difference in legislative specialization between the two houses—the abundant committee responsibilities of senators and the limited committee obligations of House members—and how this simple difference in dividing the public policy pie produces great differences on the north and south sides of the Capitol. Also looked at is how the difference in size has produced rules of procedure that vary greatly—one set that enables the leadership of the House to process legislation in a vast, populous, and specialized legislative body, and another set that produces problematical and tentative leadership on the Senate side, and a chamber much more full of surprises than the House. The rules are also a reflection of the relative value of a single member and the different emphasis placed on one's party identity and ideology in the House and Senate.

Chapter 3 deals with the very profound differences in partisanship between the two chambers with particular reference to how these differences are played out in the committees of each. Also considered is the role played by staff in the interactions among members in both chambers and the impact of the size of each body on the management of conflict.

Chapter 4 examines the electoral environments in which House members and senators compete: The first is a spatial environment, the congressional district versus the entire state. The second difference is temporal: the two-year House term versus the six-year Senate term. The various dynamics of both environments are examined in the context of congressional elections.

Distinctions have long been noted in the way journalists cover the two houses of Congress. A good deal of the evidence put forth by those who argued for a convergence of the House and Senate derived from what appeared to be a more active media style on the part of House members and a measure of success in closing the media-coverage gap that had traditionally favored the Senate. In Chapter 5 I evaluate the breadth of that gap from the perspective of the journalists.

Less well noted than the different perceptions of journalists regarding the two houses have been the distinctions made by lobbyists, the second group whose symbiosis with Congress is a critical factor in the operation of the institution. The tendency to talk about "lobbying Congress" conceals some very interesting adjustments in technique and strategy used by lobbyists when they shift their persuasive efforts from one house to the other.

Chapter 6 examines the evidence for convergence and the countervailing testimony that suggests the continued distinctiveness of the two houses. Beyond that, however, is the question of what difference these 200-year-old distinctions make even if they are demonstrated to have persisted. Do representatives and senators operate on the basis of these distinctions? Do the American people see them, and if they do see them, do they care? Is the quality of American politics enriched for the fact that its two legislative chambers retain their distinctiveness? I will try to answer some of these questions in Chapter 7 using as an example the passage of the 1986 and 1988 versions of the drug bill.

N O T E S

1. See Roger H. Davidson and Walter J. Oleszek, *Congress and Its Members,* 2d ed. (Washington, D.C.: CQ Press, 1985), p. 216; Lewis A. Froman, Jr., *The Congressional Process* (Boston: Little, Brown, 1967), pp. 7–15; and David C. Kozak, "House-Senate Differences: A Test Among Interview Data," in David C. Kozak and John D. Macartney, eds., *Congress and Public Policy* (Chicago: Dorsey Press, 1987), pp. 79–94.
2. Ibid.
3. Ibid.
4. See, for example, Norman J. Ornstein, "The New House and the New Senate," in Thomas E. Mann and Norman J. Ornstein, eds., *The New Congress* (Washington, D.C.: American Enterprise Institute, 1981).
5. William S. White, *Home Place* (Boston: Houghton-Mifflin, 1965), p. 45.

Acknowledgments

THIS BOOK IS ABOUT the two houses of the U.S. Congress, their differences, their similarities, their relationships with each other, and the current status of American bicameralism. The word that comes to mind when describing such an approach is "institutional." It is a word that conjures up an image of forbidding marble buildings in which complex and mysterious civic rituals are acted out.

But my experience, both as a political scientist and a sometime staff member who has worked in both the House and Senate, tells me that the beginning of all wisdom on the subject of Congress is that people provide the key to understanding Congress. And in the two years it took to conduct the research and write this book, it was the willingness of helpful and generous people that enabled me to fulfill the goals of the project.

The list that follows contains many names. Others might have been added except for the fact that the frankness of their answers led them to request anonymity. In appreciation for their forthrightness, I have marked their interviews "not for attribution."

Others were willing either to go on the record or to facilitate the research in other ways. Their names appear below and with their mention goes my thanks.

Donnald K. Anderson, Clerk of the U.S. House of Representatives

Richard A. Baker, Historian of the U.S. Senate

Bill Cable, Timmons & Co., Washington, D.C.

Bert Carp, Vice-President, Turner Broadcasting, Washington, D.C.

Philip Chartrand, U.S. Office of Personnel Management, Washington, D.C.

Ann Compton, ABC News

Thomas A. Dine, Director, American-Israel Public Affairs Committee, Washington, D.C.

Kenneth Duberstein, Timmons & Co., Washington, D.C.

Thomas Edsall, *Washington Post*

Peter Fenn, Fenn and King Communications, Washington, D.C.

Richard F. Fenno, Jr., Kennan Professor of Political Science, University of Rochester, Rochester, New York

Alvin From, Executive Director, Democratic Leadership Council, Washington, D.C.

Kevin Gottlieb, Washington Representative, Outdoor Advertising Association of America

Charles Green, Knight-Ridder Newspapers

Richard Hargesheimer, Legislative Council, State of Nebraska

James Hershman, U.S. Office of Personnel Management, Washington, D.C.

Patti Iglarsh, U.S. Office of Personnel Management, Washington, D.C.

Bert Levine, Vice-President, Johnson & Johnson, New Brunswick, N.J.

E. Raymond Lewis, Chief, Library of the U.S. House of Representatives

Burdett Loomis, Professor of Political Science, University of Kansas

Lawrence D. Longley, Professor of Government, Lawrence University, Appleton, Wisconsin

William T. Lyons, Director, Federal Government Relations Ciba-Geigy Corp., Washington, D.C.

Christopher Matthews, Washington Bureau Chief, *San Francisco Examiner*

Tony Mauro, Law Correspondent, *USA Today*

Harris Miller, President, Harris Miller & Associates, Arlington, Virginia

Michael W. Naylor, Director, Legislative and Regulatory Affairs, Allied-Signal, Inc.

Howard Paster, Timmons & Co., Washington, D.C.

Leroy Rieselbach, Professor of Political Science, University of Indiana

Donald A. Ritchie, Associate Historian of the U.S. Senate

Steven V. Roberts, *New York Times*

David Rubinstein, Washington, D.C.

Janice Churchill Sadeghian, Acting Director, Government Executive Institute, Washington, D.C.

Stephen A. Salmore, Eagleton Institute of Politics, Rutgers University

Raymond W. Smock, Historian, U.S. House of Representatives

Howard Stevens, U.S. Office of Personnel Management

Jane Stewart, U.S. Office of Personnel Management

Kathleen J. Tuttle, Esq., Office of the Los Angeles County District Attorney

Owen Ullman, Knight-Ridder Newspapers

Carl Van Horn, Eagleton Institute of Politics

Linda Wertheimer, National Public Radio

Special thanks and appreciation go to the following people who took a special interest in this project at times when support and wisdom were especially needed.

Barbara G. Salmore, Professor of Political Science at Drew University, read the manuscript with her trained social scientist's eye and made a number of important suggestions for improvement.

Edith Saks of the Eagleton Institute of Politics, who has been a partner in all of the projects for the past ten years, was no less indispensible on this one.

Alan Rosenthal of the Eagleton Institute of Politics at Rutgers proved once again what a good friend he was by providing early support for the project and was always available as a source of wisdom and encouragement.

Mildred Porter of the Democratic Leadership Council served as an important ally in enabling me to gain access to members of Congress.

Finally, I would like to extend my thanks to the following present and former members of the United States Senate and the United States House of Representatives:

Senator James G. Abourezk; Senator Max S. Baucus; Representative Richard Bolling; Senator John C. Culver; Senator Christopher J. Dodd; Senator J. William Fulbright; Senator Phil Gramm; Representative Floyd Fithian; Senator Wiliam Hathaway; Senator Charles Mathias; Senator George S. McGovern; Senator Edmund S. Muskie; Senator Donald W. Riegle, Jr.; Senator Abraham Ribicoff; Senator Paul S. Sarbanes; Senator Richard S. Schweiker; Senator Hugh D. Scott; Senator George A. Smathers; Senator Margaret Chase Smith; Senator Robert A. Taft, Jr.; Representative Frank Thompson; and Senator Timothy Wirth.

HOUSE
AND
SENATE

1

Two Sides of the Capitol
The Evolution of the House and Senate

REPRESENTATIVE CLARENCE CANNON (D-MO.) was a man described by one colleague as having "the air of a man smelling a rotten egg." Chairman of the House Appropriations Committee from 1949 until his death in 1964, Cannon's face—often described as "prunelike"—was seen by millions of Americans as they viewed the quadrennial Democratic Conventions, where he was a longtime parliamentarian. Once, when an opponent accused him of being two-faced, Cannon replied, "Don't you think if I had two faces I'd use the other one instead of this one?"[1]

In 1962, at the dignified age of eighty-three, Cannon became involved in an indecorous public spat with his Senate counterpart, Appropriations Committee chairman Carl Hayden (D-Ariz.), a man one year his senior who had represented his state from the very day it entered the Union in 1912. At the time of his squabble with Cannon, Hayden was also president *pro tem* of the Senate and third in line to succeed the president. Described as "quiet and manly,"[2] Hayden had the reputation for having "smiled more money through the Committee on Appropriations than any other senator has gotten by valid argument."[3]

Perhaps it was inevitable that two such different men in comparable positions in the House and Senate, and having shared custody of the spending of public funds, would ultimately clash. What was at stake in this unseemly quarrel was nothing less than the honor of the House and Senate. The event itself saw the breakdown of the appropriations process—the constitutional procedure whereby Congress provides money for the operation of the federal government.

The Bicameral Battle of the Titans

The origins of the 1962 appropriations war can be found in the bare language of Article I, Section 7, of the Constitution, which says, "All bills for raising revenue shall originate in the House of Representatives." That would seem to mean that only tax bills need originate there, but from the very earliest time the House took the institutional position that the phrase "raising revenue" should also include the making of appropriations. The reason for this position was that at the time of the writing of the U.S. Constitution the British House of Commons, upon which the U.S. House of Representatives was modeled, enjoyed the right to initiate all "money bills."[4]

At no time in history was there any question but that the Senate could freely amend any tax or spending bill when it arrived from the House, and while the Senate never challenged the House on the question of initiating tax measures, the right to move first on appropriations in the absence of House action was quite another matter.

The controversy over who got first shot at appropriations bills flared up occasionally during the nineteenth century because of the occasional failure of the House to act in a timely fashion on spending bills, with the Senate claiming the right to initiate appropriations when the House failed to take the initiative. By the end of the nineteenth century, the Senate accepted the general principle that the House would initiate the appropriations bills but reserved to itself the right to do so if the need arose. The House conceded to the Senate something that might have appeared purely symbolic but that in the delicate and subtle realm of bicameral relations was to prove important. Meetings of conference committees convened for the purpose of working out differences between House and Senate versions of the annual appropriations bills would be held on the Senate side of the Capitol and would be chaired by a senator.

A more direct influence on the struggle between the two chairmen was a practice that had grown up in Congress in the 1930s called "back-door spending," which enabled a federal agency to borrow money directly from the U.S. Treasury rather than seek a regular appropriation of Congress. Cannon regarded himself as a watchdog of the Treasury and detested the practice of back-door spending because it circumvented his committee and violated his notions of frugality. Accordingly, when the House adjourned in September 1961, one of its last acts was to pass an appropriations bill that eliminated back-door spending for four major programs.

By adjourning with the Senate still in session the House was in effect telling the Senate, "Take it or leave it." With the House in adjournment and its members back in their districts there would be no way for the Senate to get the appropriations back into the bill in a conference committee. If the Senate played hardball and took no action on the appropriations bill, the federal government would close down for lack of money, so the Senate acquiesced. "By its formal act of adjournment with so major a bill still unpassed and in disagreement, the House had profoundly insulted the Senate at one of its most sensitive points, its own prestige."[5]

But Cannon's seething resentment against the Senate was generated by more than back-door spending. There was the matter of the location of the appropriations conferences— which, for Cannon, and others of the House, symbolized the arrogance of the Senate. One senior Republican representative had complained, "The House members have to walk over to the Senate side. We don't like that at all. We've asked the Senators, 'Why don't you come over here once in a while?' but they won't."[6]

While Cannon was personally irked at the inconvenience of having to scurry (if one of his age and distinction can be said to scurry) back from appropriations conferences on the Senate

side when the buzzer for a roll-call vote on the House floor
sounded, the pique was more institutional than personal. "The
issue symbolized for House members the unfair domination
exercised by senators in relations between the houses and also
symbolized the prestige enjoyed by the upper house."[7]

Senator Joseph S. Clark, a Pennsylvania Democrat, saw in
the assertiveness of the House members an effort to downgrade
the Senate to the largely symbolic status of the British House
of Lords. "Senate resentment at this desire," Clark observed,
"is naturally fierce."[8]

The battle broke out dramatically when Congress returned
for the 1962 session, with the House led by a new Speaker, John
McCormick of Massachusetts. Chairman Cannon phoned
Chairman Hayden to inform him that henceforth House-Senate
conferences on appropriations bills would alternate in their
meeting places between the House side of the Capitol and the
Senate side and that the House Appropriations Committee had
recently adopted a resolution to that effect.

The Senate retaliated swiftly. On February 9, Chairman
Hayden called his committee into session and they voted to
accept the arrangement for alternate meeting sites on the House
and Senate sides provided that the House agree to allowing the
Senate to originate half the appropriations bills taken up each
year.[9]

The first actual test of wills took place on April 10 when a
conference committee met on the Senate side under the chairmanship of a senator. At the conclusion of the meeting, House
members announced that the next meeting would take place on
the House side under a House chairman. The meeting broke up
in angry disagreement, and for the next three months each
house passed its own appropriations bills. But since the House
and Senate chairmen could not agree on a mutually acceptable
meeting site for the next conference, there was no way to work
out the differences between the House and Senate versions of
the appropriations bills and combine them into a single piece
of legislation to be sent to the president, as the Constitution

requires. The two houses' versions of the same bill might be astonishingly close, but close is not good enough when a single bill must be presented to the president for his approval or veto.

Throughout the spring of 1962 the differences between the two chairmen went unresolved, but by the latter part of June what had been an irritating but hardly dire situation grew more ominous as the end of the fiscal year approached.

In those days, the federal government's fiscal year began on July 1 instead of the current October 1. Any agency of the federal government without money appropriated for it after June 30 would have to begin closing down. Accordingly, a desperate last-minute meeting was called by Carl Hayden, the Senate appropriations chairman. The locale chosen for the meeting underscored the delicacy of the situation. Hayden asked Cannon and his House colleagues to meet with their Senate counterparts in the old Supreme Court chamber, which was located almost precisely within the Capitol at the midpoint between the House and Senate wings, but slightly over the line on Senate terrain.

After demanding that the chairmanship of the meeting be divided between Hayden and himself, Cannon attacked the Senate's appropriations bill as spendthrift, thereby injecting a note of substance into what had thus far been a procedural and symbolic tiff. Cannon saw himself and his committee as vigilant guardians of the public's money, and the recommendations of the Appropriations Committee to the House reflected that frugality. The Senate Appropriations Committee, in contrast, was viewed by Cannon as entirely too sympathetic to the pleas of agencies of the executive branch for more funds and altogether too open-handed in appropriating money for such "frills" as foreign economic assistance and operating funds for the State Department.

Given this set of underlying differences, based largely on the peculiarities of the bicameral system, institutional positions hardened. July 1 was approaching with the prospect that 2 million federal workers would go without pay. A very disquieting plea was issued by Secret Service chief James Rowley to his agents to agree to continue protecting President Kennedy despite the cutoff in their paychecks.[10]

In the last week of June a flurry of angry letters passed between the two chairmen. Cannon wrote to Hayden criticizing the Senate for having "invariably increased every appropriations bill passed by the House." One of Hayden's colleagues characterized Cannon's accusation as "unfair and vicious." Senator A. Willis Robertson of Virginia (father of 1988 presidential hopeful Pat Robertson), who had spent seven terms in the House before coming to the Senate, accused Cannon of "insulting" the Senate by "subtly charging the Senate committee with wasting public funds." But he went beyond the mere upholding of the Senate's honor by transgressing on one of the most sensitive areas for House members. He said, "No sitting member of the Senate ever ran for election to the House of Representatives."[11]

Robertson had uttered the ineffable. His observation was tantamount to mentioning rope in the house of a hanged man. Senators might know, in their heart of hearts, that all House members hankered to be senators, but one would never be so bold as to proclaim it. The flames of intercameral warfare had been fanned and the government teetered on the brink of insolvency as House members and senators upholding the honor and dignity of their respective chambers slugged it out in public.

But communication between the House and Senate was never suspended and, despite the acerbity of their exchanges, Cannon and Hayden, who were known to be on personally friendly terms, continued to negotiate. The immediate problem of a payless government was solved by a temporary "continuing resolution" to extend the funding of existing programs past the July 1 deadline.

The more far-reaching constitutional crisis was solved in a remarkably prosaic way on July 20, 1962, when House and Senate conferees met to discuss a supplemental appropriations bill. The first order of business was a coin toss. The winner was a House member, Albert Thomas (D-Tex.), who took the chair, and for the first time in living memory a House member presided over an appropriations conference committee.[12]

What does the episode tell us about these two great deliberative bodies? It tells us that they are very different institutions and although we refer to the two, collectively, as "Congress," the components are distinct.

We see chambers of dramatically different size in which there is a prestige differential that favors the smaller house, but this situation is accompanied by a sensitivity to slights on the part of the larger body that its prerogatives be properly venerated by the more elite chamber. The size difference also produces broader responsibilities for those in the smaller body, where there are but 100 members to do the legislative work that 435 members do in the larger house.

We see that although the lawmaking power vested by the Constitution in both houses is more or less the same, there are important differences, and these differences create two quite distinct institutional personalities. At the time it was fashionable for people to refer to the Senate as the more "liberal" of the two institutions based, in large measure, on its greater open-handedness on appropriations.

Underlying the more generous disposition of the Senate were the structural and functional characteristics that set it apart from the House. The most fundamental characteristic is that senators represent broader constituencies than do House members. Senators represent entire states whose interests and populations can be extraordinarily diverse, so the senator must pay heed to a bewildering variety of voices. "A House member, who represents only a segment of a state's population, can look out for his own constituents' needs and do the bidding of the small number of interests in his own territory. For all other groups, he need show no mercy. The senator, on the other hand . . . must serve as caretaker of the interests of a wider variety of groups."[13]

Another reason for the Senate committee's generosity came

from the fact that the Senate, with fewer members than the House but the same legislative responsibilities, required senators to serve on several committees while House members usually had only one major committee assignment. Senators, accordingly, might find themselves not only members of the committee that provided the legal authorization for an agency or program but members of the Appropriations Committee that provided it with the money to operate. In a congressional system in which there are separate legislative cycles of authorization and appropriation, a senator could influence both the operating authority of an agency and the amount of money it received. "In the House, an Appropriations Committee member has no other committee. Therefore there is no interlocking directorate—the man who appropriates cannot be the one who has authorized. Therefore, slashes will be made more freely."[14]

Finally, there was the simple fact that the House acted first on appropriations bills and the Senate had the final shot at them. This made the Senate into the court of last resort for interest groups or officials of the executive branch who needed more money for their agencies. An important factor in the Senate's "liberalness" was that it often had to offset the excessive parsimony of Cannon. Over the years of Cannon's chairmanship of the House Appropriations Committee, senators had come to expect appropriations bills from the House to be stingy in the extreme. This stark structural difference no longer characterizes the positions of the two houses on spending matters, but at that time senators were prepared to add funds to their own appropriations bills that were well beyond what Cannon and his colleagues would consider prudent. The expectation on both sides of the Hill, however, was that the dollar differences would be worked out in the conference in which members of both appropriations committees would predominate.[15] So the liberal reputation enjoyed by the Senate on spending bills was largely a product of comparison to the frugal House.

We must also be mindful of the 173 years of House-Senate relationships that preceded the Cannon-Hayden showdown.

Considerable historical baggage was carried into that controversy, characterized by fluctuations in the fortunes of both chambers and in the relations between them. The adoption of a bicameral form of national legislature was an obstacle to tyranny, but with it came a measure of jealousy and conflict for the two powerful and independent institutions charged jointly with making the nation's laws.

"The Remedy for This Inconveniency"

Bicameralism was not an American idea. It had its roots in the idea of mixed government that can be traced to Aristotle and his notion of a "golden mean"—a moderate middle course between extremes. Institutionally, this expressed itself in forms of government in which power was distributed rather than concentrated. The Roman philosopher Polybius brought the concept forward in the second century B.C. and it was advanced and refined in the Middle Ages by Marsilius of Padua (*c.* 1280–*c.* 1343), who argued that the power to legislate ought to reside in the people. In the period after the Glorious Revolution (1688–1689), John Locke styled a governmental system wherein power and functions were divided as "balanced government." But the most direct influence on the framers of the Constitution was the Frenchman Baron Montesquieu (1689–1755), who warned, in *The Spirit of the Laws* (1748), against concentrating legislative and executive power in a single pair of hands. He urged that legislative power be divided between two assemblies, one of which would represent the nobility and the other the people. This arrangement, of course, was the one that prevailed in Great Britain with a Parliament consisting of a House of Commons and a House of Lords.

But when the framers of the Constitution gathered in Philadelphia in 1787, they realized that Montesquieu's persuasive theory and Great Britain's admirable practice did not readily fit the American situation. Bicameralism in both was based upon representing the common people, which we had, and the

aristocracy, which we did not have. Manufacturing an aristocracy in order to emulate British practice or Montesquieuan
theory was not a serious possibility. Legislative power was
greatly feared by these early framers because of their experience
with a powerful British Parliament, but devising a basis for
dividing legislative power between two chambers in a nation
without a hereditary nobility was a test of the ingenuity of even
this remarkable collection of men who participated in the constitutional debate. Indeed, the greatest single controversy at the
Constitutional Convention took place over the composition and
mode of selection of the second chamber. Should the upper
chamber be selected by the lower? Should the people participate
directly in the selection or election of senators? What role
should the state legislatures play in the selection of senators?

The practice of the thirteen states and their own legislatures
was even more compelling than the writings of Locke and
Montesquieu or the example of the British Parliament. The
constitutions of ten of the states had established bicameral legislatures, but neither the Continental Congress that had functioned during the War of Independence nor the Articles of the
Confederation Congress that succeeded it had been bicameral.
That seems, however, to have been considered a mistake, and
there was little enthusiasm for a one-house legislature at the
Constitutional Convention, except in the Pennsylvania delegation. The agenda-setting Virginia Plan put forth by Edmund
Randolph called for two legislative houses. Randolph's plan,
however, called for a lower house elected by the people which
would, in turn, elect an upper house.

New Jersey's rejoinder on behalf of smaller and less populous states was that all states enjoy equality of representation
in a single-house Congress that would choose the executive.
This proposal was rejected but the idea of having at least one
house of Congress in which all states had the same number of
seats was a rallying point for the smaller states and forced the
Convention to appoint a committee to come up with a compromise. On July 16, 1787, by a one-vote margin, the Convention

approved the committee's recommendation: In return for a Senate in which all states would have an equal vote, the House would be empowered to initiate revenue bills.[16]

So vitally important was the question of how representation would be determined in Congress that the Convention would probably have collapsed over failure to resolve it. Ratification, however, did not turn on the question; rather, the enduring concern of Americans was that Congress, as the branch of the national government with sweeping lawmaking powers, be deterred from using those powers for tyrannical ends. Bicameralism and a system of checks and balances made legislative despotism less likely. While required by the Constitution to cooperate in general legislation, each house was made—by reason of its diverse powers, different constituencies, and varying terms and methods of election—into a highly distinctive body. Just how distinctive was expressed by James Madison as he observed, "In republican government, the legislative authority necessarily predominates. The remedy for this inconveniency is, to divide the legislature into different branches; and to render them, by different modes of election, and different principles of action, as little connected with each other, as the nature of their common functions and their common dependence on the society, will admit."[17]

The device for dealing with this "inconveniency" was to produce two legislative bodies that differed starkly at their creation and had an enduring rivalry encoded in their constitutional makeup.

If the Constitution's framers looked warily on the institutions they had created, their greatest uneasiness concerned the House of Representatives. Elected by the people directly, it possessed a democratic legitimacy that was enjoyed neither by the presidency, which had the electoral college interposed between it and the citizens, nor by the Senate, whose members were chosen by the state legislatures. Anticipating a high turnover in House membership because of the briefness of these legislators' terms and the arduousness of travel to and from the seat of government, Madison concluded that the Speaker of the House would emerge as a formidable figure. He reasoned that with so few House members willing to "become members of long standing" and "masters of the public business," a resourceful Speaker would dominate a transient membership since few would ever learn enough about the institution to challenge him. Unlike the House, the Senate would have no powerful presiding officer. The vice-president designated by the Constitution to preside over the Senate would lack the legitimacy that came from direct election by the people. Accordingly, "the House seemed destined to be the most prestigious and powerful body because of its elective status, its pre-eminence in fiscal matters, and its presumed capacity to generate strong and forceful leadership."[18]

The Senate was perceived in a far different light. Reflecting upon the early history of Congress seventy years after ratification, Vice-President John Breckinridge said, "At the origin of the government, the Senate seemed to be regarded as an executive council. The president often visited the chamber and conferred personally with his body; most of its business was transacted with closed doors and it took comparatively little part in legislative debates. The rising and vigorous intellects of the country sought the arena of the House of Representatives as the appropriate theater for the display of their powers." Indeed, "in December 1790 when [James] Monroe . . . took his seat in the Senate, the upper chamber could aptly be described as a graveyard of talent. . . . Like the Confederation Congress, the Senate held its sessions . . . under a self-imposed rule of secrecy. The public knew little of what went on other than the meager information garnered from the bare record of the journal. Since the members had no opportunity to dazzle the people with their oratory, attention was concentrated on the House of Representatives, where full publicity was given to proceedings."[19]

But even after future president James Monroe argued successfully to open Senate debates to the public in 1794, the upper chamber continued in the shadow of the House.

Certainly the accounts of the early nineteenth century reflect an image of a Senate as a kind of stuffy, somnolent, and semi-secret society with little to do or say. A lugubrious entry in the diary of Senator John Quincy Adams for the last day of 1805 reflects the inactivity of life in the Senate: "The year which this day expires has been distinguished in the course of my life by its barrenness of events."[20]

Adams served only a single, unhappy term in the Senate. Entries in his diary suggest that he must have found debate in the House of Representatives more engrossing than that in his own chamber because he seems to have spent a good deal of time there. His Senate career ended abruptly and unpleasantly when the Massachusetts legislature chose his successor well in advance of the end of his term. It was a rebuke to Adams over his support of President Thomas Jefferson's foreign policy.

Adams went on to a career as a diplomat that culminated in his selection as Secretary of State. In 1824 he became president in an election so close it was decided in the House. Embittered at his failure to win a second term, Adams believed his public career had come to an end. But within six months of leaving the White House, Adams was visited by Representative Joseph Richardson, who represented the district in Massachusetts that included the ex-president's ancestral home. Richardson had decided not to seek another term in the House and urged Adams to run for his seat. Richardson told Adams that service "in the House of Representatives of an ex-president of the United States, instead of degrading the individual, would elevate the Representative character."[21] It is in some degree a measure of the prestige the House enjoyed that Adams agreed, saying, "I had no scruple whatever. No person could be degraded by serving the people as a Representative in Congress."[22]

It was in the House that Adams achieved his greatest distinction in public life. He had found the place where his talents could be expressed. He served just ten days short of seventeen years in the House, where he spoke out boldly against slavery. And it was on the floor of the House that Adams suffered the final paralytic stroke that ended his life.

Examining the political careers of some of the most notable

figures of the first quarter of the nineteenth century one finds
that they were as likely to leave the Senate for the House as they
were to abandon the House for the Senate.

Henry Clay of Kentucky, one of Adams's rivals for the
presidency in 1824 and founder and standard-bearer of the
Whig Party, also moved from a seat in the Senate to one in
the House, stating that he wished to be "an immediate representative of the people." In the House Clay was elected Speaker
in his freshman year in 1811 and became a leading "war hawk"
in that chamber in urging hostilities against Great Britain.

The fact that Clay, a man known for his political astuteness,
returned to the Senate in 1831 reveals much about the change
in the status of the upper chamber. In the early years of the
century when Monroe and Adams served there, senators were
relatively inactive: They introduced less legislation than did
House members, participated less in committee activities, and
often did not even serve out a full six-year term. They were
often under the thumbs of the legislatures that had elected
them, and even the newspapers paid less attention to them than
they did to members of the House. In 1805, for example, House
activities accounted for 27 percent of newspaper space in a
sample of papers of the day; Senate activities for the same
period garnered only about 3 percent.[23] By 1830, however, the
Senate was taking its place alongside the House as an equal
partner and, in some estimations, was poised to surpass it.

The Rise of the Senate

The rise of the Senate was well under way by the middle of
the 1820s. The great debate that culminated in the Missouri
Compromise in 1820 was discussed as fully and as publicly in
the Senate as it had been in the House, and the possibilities
inherent in the six-year term began to be seen as political advantages in light of the balancing out of other differences. This
change was first seen in the increased gravitation of promising
national leaders like Clay to the Senate. By the 19th Congress

(1825–1827), the Senate was full of future presidents: Andrew Jackson, Martin Van Buren, and Benjamin Harrison were in the upper chamber along with such future notables as William R. King, who became vice-president in 1853, Robert V. Hayne, who would engage Daniel Webster in a classic set of Senate debates, and Thomas Hart Benton, whose influence would extend over an unprecedented thirty years of Senate service.

· It was at about this time that Alexis de Tocqueville visited the United States and in the course of his extensive observations of the institutions and mores of America contrasted the House and Senate.

On entering the House of Representatives of Washington one is struck by the vulgar demeanor of that great assembly. The eye frequently does not discover a man of celebrity within its walls . . .

At a few yards' distance from this spot is the door of the Seante, which contains within a small space a large proportion of the most celebrated men of America. . . . The Senate is composed of eloquent advocates, distinguished generals, wise magistrates, and statemen of note, whose language would at all times do honour to the most remarkable parliamentary debates of Europe.[24]

Tocqueville, with his dread of popular tyranny, could hardly be expected to embrace the House. He ascribed the superiority of the Senate to the election of its members by the state legislatures, which caused the Senate, in his estimation, "to represent the elevated thoughts which are current in the community . . . rather than the petty passions which disturb or the vices which disgrace it."[25] To Tocqueville, the House, with its direct election by the people, represented these "petty passions" and "vices."

But it was Tocqueville's characterizations of House members as "mostly village lawyers" and "people [who] do not always know how to read correctly" and his description of senators as enjoying "a monopoly of intelligence and of sound judgment" that occasioned a spirited rejoinder from Thomas

Hart Benton, who recalled for the otherwise-opinioned French aristocrat something obvious that he had overlooked.

[Tocqueville] seems to look upon the members of the two Houses as different orders of beings—different classes—a higher and a lower class; the former placed in the Senate by the wisdom of state legislatures, the latter in the House of Representatives by the folly of the people—when the fact is that they are not only of the same order and class, but mainly the same individuals. The Senate is almost entirely made up of the House! and it is quite certain that every senator whom Mons. de Tocqueville had in his eye when he bestowed such encomium on that body had come from the House of Representatives![26]

That a thoughtful observer had placed the Senate above the House would have surprised the framers of the Constitution. Even Benton's vindication of the House might have struck them as a trifle defensive. What was happening was an equalizing of the statures that was not foreseen in 1787. Tocqueville was correct in his appraisal of the quality of senators, as was Benton in his rejoinder that "the Senate is in great part composed of the pick of the House, and therefore gains double—by brilliant accession to itself and abstraction from the other."[27]

It was, however, the playing out of the inevitable consequences of the greater formula for representation in the House that contributed most to the rise of the Senate. "While the large increase in the number of representatives had forced the adoption of rules that inhibited the role and opportunities for debate in the House, the growth of the Senate to a membership of almost fifty had worked to the contrary, making it a more lively and rewarding forum for those who wanted to lead and be heard. Moreover, the equality of state representation in the Senate, and the growing concern over divisions between the free and slave states that had been underscored by the Missouri controversy, heightened the Senate's importance as the arena in which southerners could block the action of an antagonistic House majority."[28]

At 183 members in the 17th Congress that convened after the census of 1820, the House had swelled to almost four times the size of the Senate, from less than three times its size in the 1st Congress (1789–1791). This growth in size was marked by a tightening of the rules of debate so that by 1841 House members were limited to one hour of debate and by 1847 a Five Minute Rule was imposed. Even the physical arrangements of the Senate chamber seemed to promote high-quality debate: "The small, semicircular Senate chamber, with plain walls and a domed roof, had excellent acoustics and was ideal for the ringing voices of eloquent men."[29]

The nature of American public policy was also changing in a way that favored the Senate over the House. So long as the United States was an isolated agricultural society preoccupied with domestic problems, the mainstream of policy consisted of the development of interstate commerce, internal improvements (such as roads and canals), and the revenues for defraying their cost. Foreign policy for a small and struggling nation was defined not in terms of grand alliances and broad diplomatic initiatives but rather in terms of trade and tariff policy—the domain of the House with its primacy in fiscal matters. Grand diplomatic strokes—the purchase of the Louisiana Territory from France and the proclamation of the Monroe Doctrine—were presidential in origin, infrequent, and not the subject of determined senatorial opposition. As mentioned, the Senate did emerge as the forum for debate on the question of slavery. At a political disadvantage in a House of Representatives where the more populous states dominated, the sparsely populated slave states chose the Senate with its equality of state representation as their first and last line of defense.[30]

The period of the Senate's rise to parity with the House extended through the Civil War and into the late nineteenth century. It was a period of dominance by the two chambers over the executive branch, "a golden era for the bicameral Congress. . . . Both the House and Senate possessed constitutional powers that were critical to national policymaking, and both were well organized. Each asserted its unique constitutional powers and played a clear role in making national policy."[31]

This period of bicameral parity was celebrated in 1885 by the young scholar Woodrow Wilson as an era of bicameral amity as well. "There is safety and ease," he wrote, "in the fact that the Senate never wishes to carry its resistance to the House to the point at which resistance must stay all progress in legislation; because there is really a 'latent unity' between the Senate and the House which makes continued antagonism between them next to impossible—certainly in the highest degree improbable."[32]

Wilson argued forcefully against the accusations of reformers that the Senate was a millionaire's club assembled by state legislatures that were, themselves, under the thumb of powerful economic interests. His defense was that of the classic pluralist: They may be millionaires but the interests they represent are so varied—and indeed often so antagonistic—that their wealth does not constitute a consistent upper-class interest. He assured his readers that "the Senate is quite as trustworthy in this regard as is the House of Representatives."[33]

It was during this period that the mode of electing senators came under attack by reformers who urged that popular election supplant selection by the state legislatures. The House had voted five times over a nine-year period, between 1893 and 1902, for a constitutional amendment requiring direct popular election of senators—twice by the constitutionally required two-thirds vote—but between 1902 and 1911 all such efforts ceased. The leadership of the House considered it a waste of time to persist in passing such amendments only to have them foiled in the Senate. But beginning with Oregon in 1901, states began to have nonbinding senatorial primaries that were, in effect, advice to state legislatures on who was the peoples' choice for the U.S. Senate. Finally, in 1911 under the leadership of Senator William Borah of Idaho the amendment passed the Senate by a two-thirds vote; it was quickly ratified by three-fourths of the states and went into effect on May 31, 1913, as the Seventeenth Amendment.[34]

The direct election of senators removed the one conspicuous disadvantage that had afflicted the Senate from its beginnings: lack of democratic legitimacy. The Senate retained its distinctive powers of advice and consent in treaties and presidential appointments and, above all, its compact size. At the time of ratification of the Seventeenth Amendment the number of House members had reached its present number of 435 while the size of the Senate was 96. Internal reforms in the House that had curbed the power of the Speaker made leadership of the larger body somewhat more uncertain. But it was a change in the content of American public policy in the World War I period that propelled the Senate ahead of the House.

The great national debates over American entry into World War I took place in the Senate. It was in the Senate that President Woodrow Wilson battled the "small group of willful men" who in 1917 opposed his plan to arm U.S. merchant vessels to protect them against German submarines. Only in the Senate could Wilson's opponents, through the use of the extreme form of extended debate, the filibuster, derail the armed-ship bill.

The Versailles Treaty was also fought on the floor of the Senate. The treaty, which would have provided for U.S. membership in the League of Nations, was defeated in large measure because of President Wilson's failure to consult the Senate adequately during his negotiations on the pact. The vote to reject the Versailles Treaty revealed more clearly than had any other vote the power of the Senate in foreign policy. The entry of the United States, albeit reluctantly, into the affairs of the world signaled a shift in public policy to an area where the Senate enjoyed special powers.

By the end of World War I, it was axiomatic that Senate service was to be preferred over House service. A third of the membership of the Senate had previously served in the House and even House Speaker Champ Clark, who wielded the gavel from 1911 to 1919, enumerated crisply the advantage of the Senate.

There are various reasons why Representatives desire translation to the Senate: First, the longer term; second, Senators being fewer, their votes are more important; third, patronage; fourth, participation in treaty-making; fifth, greater social recognition.[35]

When Lord Bryce evaluated the American institutions of government at roughly the same time, he gave a measured but unmistakable advantage to the Senate.

The Senate has been a stouter bulwark against agitation, not merely because a majority of the senators have always four years of member-ship before them, but also because the senators have been individually stronger men than the representatives. They are less democratic, not in opinion but in temper, because they are more self-confident, be-cause they have more to lose, because experience has taught them how fleeting a thing popular sentiment is, and how useful a thing continu-ity in policy is. The Senate has therefore usually kept its head better than the House of Representatives. It has expressed more adequately the judgment, as contrasted with the emotion, of the nation.[36]

House reforms and the tendency of House members to make careers in that chamber tended to weaken the power of the leadership of the House. Senate reforms and careerism changed that body far less. The adoption of Senate Rule 22 did provide an easier mechanism to terminate excessive debate with a vote of cloture, but it proved so difficult to muster the required two-thirds majority needed to terminate debate that filibuster-ing was not seriously hindered. Between 1917 and the beginning of the administration of Franklin D. Roosevelt in 1933, a mere eleven votes of cloture were taken. Of that eleven only four were successful in shutting off debate.[37]

The rise of radio as the first truly national medium, along with news magazines, was a development that enhanced the Senate more than the House. "These mass media were drawn to the Senate because of its small size, which allowed them to focus on individual senators, and because the senators' large constituencies and more national and international focus provided the media with a wider audience. Media attention made national personalities out of senators and a notable debating forum out of the Senate. Individual senators and the Senate as a body could convey their opinions to the public more easily than could the larger House and its more parochial and anonymous members."[38]

The leadership of the House was particularly hobbled by the consequences of some of the reforms of the Progressive Era. One important reform removed the Speaker from the chairmanship of the Rules Committee, which specifies the conditions under which all bills are debated and amended. Unlike the Senate system of unanimous consent, which involves consultation between the leaders and interested senators on the terms of debate and amendment, the House had formalized this crucial gatekeeping function in its Rules Committee. And it was mainly through this committee that such powerful Speakers as Thomas B. Reed, a Maine Republican (1889–1891 and 1895–1899), and Joseph G. Cannon, an Illinois Republican (1903–1911), established virtual dictatorships over the House. The separation of the leadership of the Rules Committee from the Speakership created the conditions for a powerful rival to the Speaker. But this did not occur immediately. During the period between 1937 and 1960, when conservative southern Democrats occupied the Rules chair, the committee and the party leadership of the House "operated independently and often at cross-purposes."[39]

The Senate has never vested great formal power in its leaders; even a Speakership reduced in prerogatives is more imposing an office than anything in the Senate. But the Senate, befitting the deference it pays to the individual, has yielded leadership to strong individuals only occasionally. The strength of this leadership, however, rests more on the force of personality and intellect than on legal authority. Perhaps the most powerful figure in the Senate in the early years of the twentieth

century was Senator Nelson W. Aldrich (R-R.I.), whose highest formal post was chairman of the Finance Committee. Between Aldrich, who left the Senate in 1911, and Lyndon B.
Johnson (D-Tex.), who became the Democrats' floor leader in
1953, there was no single individual who was able to amass
much more personal power. During this period power sometimes resided in the hands of a few powerful committee chairmen. At other times, such as the early period of the New Deal
from 1933 until 1937, the influence of a president was greater
than that of any senator or group of senators. It was Johnson,
however, with his combination of political astuteness, utter
ruthlessness, luck, and hard work, who commanded the Senate
until he left to be John F. Kennedy's running mate in 1960.

Johnson's success was often attributed to the "treatment"
he visited upon senators who would not go along with the
meticulously fashioned deals he would engineer, but the singu-
larity of his success had more to do with his deep understanding
of the Senate than of the forcefulness of his persuasion.

Johnson, a former member of the House, understood how
profoundly the Senate differs from the House. The House, for
all the years Johnson was there, was in the control of the
Democrats. Indeed, when Johnson arrived in the House in
1937, it was in the wake of the Democratic landslide in the 1936
presidential election, and the number of Republican members
had shrunk to 89 while the Democrats held 333 seats. Thirteen
minor party members filled out the membership of the chamber. Republican senators had dwindled to 17. Nonetheless, Senate opponents of the efforts of Democratic president Franklin
D. Roosevelt to enlarge the Supreme Court to dilute the power
of conservative justices managed to defeat the president at the
peak of his power and popularity.

Roosevelt was defeated not by the anemic ranks of the
Republicans, but by a bipartisan coalition composed of conservative (typically southern) Democrats and Republicans. It was
a coalition that would persist until the early 1960s. Johnson
understood that a bare majority of 218 votes would guarantee

victory in the House, but in the Senate, with its filibuster that, at the time, could be shut down only with a two-thirds vote, a different logic prevailed. Minorities, be they partisan or ideological, could stop the Senate in its tracks. Fashioning bipartisan coalitions was Johnson's special skill and it was based on his deep and subtle understanding of senators and how they differed from House members. As Johnson's longtime aide George Reedy recalled, "There are few issues that can command majorities in and of themselves. Bills become law because of delicate trades."[40] These trades, such as those fashioned by Johnson, were based upon "the art of pitting the left and right against each other and coming through the middle."[41] It is the fashioning of consensus by accommodating all interested senators and the concerns they represent. It is the senators as individuals rather than as partisans that is crucial in this process of adjustment and accommodation. It would seem axiomatic that a common sense of purpose befitting an arm of the national legislature would be lost in such a welter of special pleadings. But what might appear, at first blush, to be an adversary process can often act as a unifying force. The building of temporary majorities in the Senate is a process that is particular in form but, on many occasions, universal in result.

Jane Mansbridge uses the terms "adversary" and "unitary" to identify two models of democracy. The adversary expression of democracy is characterized by an emphasis on representing faithfully and meticulously the various interests in one's constituency. Unitary democracy, in contrast, emphasizes the overall good and the national welfare.[42] These models are closely related to the distinctions made by the eighteenth-century British philosopher Edmund Burke, who urged the electors of Bristol to look upon Parliament as "a deliberative assembly, one nation with one interest, that of the whole; where not local purposes, not local prejudices ought to guide, but the general good, resulting from the general reason of the whole."

Two Houses, Two Democracies

This book, in making the case that vital differences between the House and Senate persist, will also suggest that the characteristics of adversary democracy are most commonly found in the House of Representatives and those of unitary democracy more typically in the Senate, and that both of these expressions of democracy are crucial to the survival of free government in America. Each model carries with it certain strengths and weaknesses, but these strengths and weaknesses are essentially complementary.

I will attempt to present a picture of an astonishingly accessible House of Representatives in which members act to solve problems that are complex and daunting for the ordinary citizen and to defend vigilantly the interests of roughly half a million Americans. I will also sketch a Senate in which representational concerns are increasing but which retains a more national perspective. While it is difficult to demonstrate that Senate legislation is somehow more "national" than House legislation, we shall see from the testimony of fourteen senators that most think the Senate, to use Burke's words, is more likely to reflect "the general reason of the whole." This broader world view is, as I see it, the product of the ability of senators in the intimacy of a 100-member body to experience their colleagues as people rather than as partisans or brokers for interest groups.

House members, who lack statewide constituencies, represent fewer interests and any given interest is likely to loom more imposingly in a House member's calculations than that of a single interest in a large complex state. House members may be said to reflect more directly the interests of their constituencies, and they provide an important link between citizens and their government that senators cannot provide. In a mass society where expanding governmental activity threatens to engulf citizens and render them helpless, the intimate relations between House members and the voters of these 435 manageable congressional districts serve to limit the estrangement suffered by people. The almost tactile sense of knowing what made their districts tick was a powerful memory in the minds of the senators I interviewed when they recalled their days in the House and may be an important force in limiting citizens' isolation from their government.

If senators and House members perceive and express these differences between members of each house and their obligations to their constituencies and to the nation, so do Americans. Later in this book I will make note of some recent public opinion results that suggest that citizens look upon senators and representatives as doing different things and being responsive to different constituencies.

The starting point in the examination of the differences between the House and Senate and of the meaning of those differences to American democracy begins with a very basic distinction: the number of members in each house.

NOTES

1. Richard Bolling, *House Out of Order* (New York: E.P. Dutton, 1965), p. 91.
2. Harry McPherson, *A Political Education* (Boston: Little, Brown, 1972), p. 36.
3. Warren Weaver, *Both Your Houses* (New York: Praeger, 1972), p. 33.
4. George Rothwell Brown, *The Leadership of Congress* (Indianapolis: Bobbs-Merrill, 1922), p. 238.
5. Neil MacNeil, *Forge of Democracy* (New York: David McKay, 1963), p. 397.
6. Richard F. Fenno, Jr., *The Power of the Purse* (Boston: Little, Brown, 1966), p. 637.
7. Jeffrey L. Pressman, *House vs. Senate* (New Haven, Conn.: Yale University Press, 1966), p. 83.
8. Joseph S. Clark, *Congress: The Sapless Branch,* rev. ed. (New York: Harper and Row, 1965), p. 136.
9. MacNeil, op. cit., p. 398.
10. Ibid., p. 399.
11. Ibid., p. 400.
12. Weaver, op. cit., p. 33.
13. Pressman, op. cit., p. 86.
14. Ibid., p. 87.
15. Ibid., p. 88.
16. *Origins and Development of Congress* (Washington, D.C.: Congressional Quarterly Press, 1976), pp. 32–35.
17. Federalist #51 in *The Federalist* (Washington, D.C.: Thompson and Homans, 1831), p. 224.
18. Edward G. Carmines and Lawrence C. Dodd, "Bicameralism in Congress: The

Changing Partnership," in Lawrence C. Dodd and Bruce I. Oppenheimer, eds., *Congress Reconsidered,* 3d ed. (Washington, D.C.: CQ Press, 1985), p. 417.

19. Harry Ammon, *James Monroe: The Quest for National Identity* (New York: McGraw-Hill, 1971), p. 82.
20. Allan Nevins, ed., *The Diary of John Quincy Adams* (New York: Longmans, Green, 1928), p. 27.
21. Ibid., p. 405.
22. Ibid.
23. See Elaine Swift, *Reconstitutive Congressional Change: The Case of the United States Senate, 1789–1841,* unpublished doctoral thesis, Harvard University, 1989.
24. Alexis de Tocqueville, *Democracy in America,* v. 1, trans. by Henry Reeve (London: Longmans, Green, 1875), pp. 203–204.
25. Ibid.
26. Thomas Hart Benton, *Thirty Years' View,* v. 1 (New York: Appleton & Co., 1854), p. 206.
27. Ibid.
28. Alvin M. Josephy, Jr., *On the Hill: A History of the American Congress* (New York: Simon and Schuster, 1979), p. 159.
29. Ibid., p. 166.
30. Carmines and Dodd, op. cit., p. 419, and *Origins and Development of Congress,* p. 186.
31. Carmines and Dodd, op. cit., p. 420.
32. Woodrow Wilson, *Congressional Government* (Boston: Houghton-Mifflin, 1885), p. 224.
33. Ibid.
34. George H. Haynes, *The Senate of the United States* (Boston: Houghton-Mifflin, 1938), pp. 86–95.
35. Champ Clark, *My Quarter Century of American Politics,* v. 1 (New York: Harper & Bros., 1920), p. 219.
36. Viscount James Bryce, *The American Commonwealth,* v. 1 (New York: Macmillan, 1928), pp. 124–125.
37. *Origins and Development of Congress,* pp. 226–227.
38. Carmines and Dodd, op. cit., p. 423.
39. U.S. Congress, House, *A History of the Committee on Rules,* 97th Congress, 2d Session, 1983, p. 177.
40. George E. Reedy, *The U.S. Senate* (New York: Crown, 1986), p. 126.
41. Ibid., p. 205.
42. Jane J. Mansbridge, *Beyond Adversary Democracy* (Chicago: University of Chicago Press, 1983).

2

Politics of Scale

The Size Difference

W E MIGHT NOT EXPECT a group of fourteen present and former senators of different parties, ideol-
ogies, and regions of the country to express near-
unanimity on a question relating to the nature of Congress, but
one question put to them brought out that very high level of
agreement.

I asked the senators who had previously served in the House
what, in their opinion, was the most important difference between the House and Senate. Twelve of the fourteen cited the
difference in size of the two houses. The two who did not point
to the vast size of the House membership and the compactness
of the Senate disagreed between themselves as to what was the
most fundamental difference: One cited the special powers conferred on the Senate by the Constitution, such as the ratification
of treaties and confirmation of presidential appointments; the
other cited the senators' six-year terms.

Now fourteen senators is not a large group, but that
twelve of them, without prompting, would cite size as the
most salient factor suggests the importance of this simple element in understanding the difference between these two institutions and why, despite some evidence in recent years that
they are becoming more alike, the two can never entirely be
congruent or identical.

The number of senators who said size, however, is less
impressive than the categorical quality of their statements. For

former senator John C. Culver, an Iowa Democrat, who spent ten years in the House and gained a reputation as a thoughtful and aggressive lawmaker in his one term in the Senate, his identification of the size factor was the most unequivocal:

I think the starting point of wisdom on comparing the House and Senate is frankly a very simple but, I believe, critical observation. That's the difference in size.

Size really explains so much else about those institutions in terms of their organization, in terms of their rules, in terms of the accessibility and participation of the members, the committees, the workloads and so forth.

More lyrical, perhaps, but no less emphatic, is the verdict of former senator Hugh D. Scott, a Pennsylvania Republican who spent sixteen years in the House and seventeen years in the Senate and who served as minority leader of the Senate. Scott observed:

The House is a massive creature. A huge overgrown elephant, but rarely turning into a rogue elephant. It's more lethargic, maybe more like a hippopotamus—a sort of hulking, sulking creature, barely showing its snout and only then when required for reasons of sustenance or curiosity.

Sustaining his zoological simile, Scott likened the Senate to

a group of people of various species like antelope or deer who leap with some grace from subject to subject, issue to issue. There is a great deal more grace of movement in a herd of antelope than in a group of hippopotamuses.

Size, as an element of House-Senate comparison, has many ramifications and implications. One obvious outgrowth of the difference in size is a stark difference in the rules that govern each chamber. A second is the degree of specialization that a senator or House member can achieve. Put another way, it means that the populous House and the tiny Senate must cover the same vast areas of public policy ranging from agriculture to space exploration. They must develop policy, legislate in identical areas, and oversee its implementation. But the House has 435 people to assign to the task and the Senate only 100. This results in vast disparities in the degree of expertise achievable between senators and members. The corollary is that there is also a vast disparity in the breadth and sweep of what senators and House members can authoritatively speak out on.

The relationship between leaders and followers in large and small organizations is different. Large organizations tend to be hierarchical and efficient at processing routine tasks. Small groups tend toward more face-to-face contact between leaders and followers with individual expressions tolerated and even encouraged. Leadership in the small body becomes more problematical.

The starting point for the examination of the size question is to make a few observations about the places where the Senate and House conduct their business.

The Ecology of the House and Senate

The House chamber is not simply large, it is the largest parliamentary room in the world. It is three times larger than the British House of Commons upon which it was patterned.[1] Paneled in walnut and trimmed with marble, the room is dominated by the Speaker's desk atop a three-tiered dais. From his seat the Speaker looks out upon a chamber in which Republicans sit to his left, Democrats to his right. Aside from this demarcation, there are no other assigned places although the floor leaders of both parties address the House from behind tables on either side of the main aisle.

The House abandoned separate desks for each member in 1912 after the members from the newly admitted states of Arizona and New Mexico were sworn in and the chamber became too crowded. But the long, padded, curved benches are not simply filled randomly by whatever person happens in. The center rear of the chamber on the Democratic side has tended to be the favorite of conservative Democrats from the Sunbelt states. The Pennsylvania delegation tends to congregate at the far right of the chamber.[2]

The Senate chamber is much different. It is small (only 125 feet at its widest) and considerably more elegant. In amphitheater style, the floor steps down in five levels toward the front of the room where the floor leaders' desks are located. As in the House, the presiding officer faces Republicans on the left and Democrats on the right, but unlike the informal seating arrangement for members, senators are assigned particular seats based upon their seniority. The general rule is to go for the "prime real estate"—seats located on either side of the center aisle, which is within the line of vision of the presiding officer. Senators located here can gain recognition to speak more easily than those located on the flanks or at the rear of the chamber.[3]

But little in the Senate is as straightforward as it appears, and many senators whose seniority would entitle them to claim "prime real estate" make individualistic—even quirky—decisions as to where they will sit. The introduction of television seems to have altered the seating calculus for some senators. Given the steep camera angle, senators with bald spots are apt to avoid the front rows. The back row may well be the new "prime real estate" for media-minded senators. The dun-colored walls do not offer a very attractive background, but there is room for a senator to set up an easel with a display and the camera angle favors certain locations in the back row.[4]

Sentiment, however, can play as important a role as telegenics. Senator Edward M. Kennedy sits in the seat occupied by his brother John F. Kennedy when the late president was a senator. Senator Margaret Chase Smith of Maine aggressively sought the desk of Vice-President Hannibal Hamlin, who had been a senator from her state. Senator Norris Cotton of New Hampshire went so far as to practice deception to claim for New Hampshire the desk of Daniel Webster, who was born in that state but represented Massachusetts in the Senate. When the two Massachusetts senators were absent one day in 1974, Cotton introduced Senate Resolution 467, 93rd Congress, 2d

Session, which required that the Webster desk be forever assigned to a senator from New Hampshire, thus snatching it from the Massachusetts delegation.[5]

A great deal was once made of the Senate phenomenon of "seatmates"—members whose fondness for one another caused them to sit together year after year. While some evidence of this remains—such as the "fun bunch," consisting of, among others, Senators Donald W. Riegle, Jr. (D-Mich.), and Jim Sasser (D-Tenn.), and a kind of inverse snobbery that has such influential senators as Ernest F. Hollings (D-S.C.) and Richard Lugar (R-Ind.) seated in the back rows of their respective sections—friendship seems a less decisive factor than it once was.[6] A conclusion based on interviews with twenty-five senators in the late 1970s would probably be reinforced by the advent of Senate television:

As is the case with so many things in the modern Senate, personal advantage and convenience rather than personal affection or even philosophical solidarity tend to provide better explanations for seat choice.[7]

The distinctive, even privileged, status of senators in contrast with House members can also be seen in the places where Congress works as well as where they speak and vote. In the three House and three Senate office buildings are subtle and not-so-subtle indications of a differential in status based on numbers.

It is manifestly more difficult to find comfortable office space for 435 members than for 100 senators. Accordingly, no senator, however junior, suffers as many limitations on space and amenities as does the newly elected House member. For one thing, each senator receives a basic space allocation of 4,000 square feet. To this an amount of up to 900 additional square feet may be added to the suites of senators from the most populous states. A House member might find himself or herself with as little as 1,000 square feet, which amounts to two rooms 25 by 20 feet each. The most spacious House office is 1,800

square feet. Greater disparities are found in the accommoda-
tions between the most senior and most junior members of the
House rather than in the Senate.[8]

At the highest level, the difference in personal space between the senator and House member evens out somewhat with
the addition of the so-called "hideaway offices" located in the
Capitol building. These suites assigned to the most senior members of both chambers bring the formal leadership of the two
bodies into rough equivalence. But there is an overall difference
that cannot escape the discerning eye when it scans Capitol
Hill. There is, for example, a huge difference in comforts and
refinements between the newest House office building (Rayburn) and the oldest (Cannon). The least senior members face
the unpleasant choice of an office on the fifth floor of Cannon
or the sixth floor of the Longworth Building.

The Cannon quarters lack the good elevator service of the
lower floors and resound with the noise of ventilating equip-
ment. But these suites are often preferred to the smaller accom-
modations in Longworth that are also afflicted with the poorest
views.

The largest suite in the Rayburn Building would not be
scorned by the chief executive officer of a corporation. That
office, 1,800 square feet, has the feel of a basketball court. The
room, 2314 Rayburn, is now occupied by Representative Jamie
Whitten (D-Miss.), who is chairman of the Appropriations
Committee.[9] But, like so much in politics, Whitten was forced
to make a trade-off in office amenities: His office has a rather
ordinary view of the "horsehoe"—the driveway on the east side
of the building—rather than the more picturesque northern
view dominated by the Capitol building.

Where seniority entitles them to have some choice over
where their office suite is located, House members often show
the same inclination to be with friends as they do in their choice
of where to sit during sessions on the floor. One is often struck
by a corridor in the Longworth Building in which it seems that
every office is occupied by a Texan. Such patterns are not so

evident on the Senate side, where more idiosyncratic factors seem to govern the location of offices. House members sometimes choose to live and work adjacent to friends. Personal friends such as Representatives Marty Russo (D-Ill.) and George Miller (D-Cal.) share an apartment on Capitol Hill and are also Rayburn Building neighbors. A basketball-playing and pizza-eating buddy of theirs, Representative Thomas Downey (D-N.Y.), has an office suite close by. Group solidarity appears to play a much more important role in the ecological choices of House members than it does of senators, but if the vast expanses of the House membership promote the hiving off of small groups of friends, it is also true that the entire membership is unknowable to the individual member.

Where one chooses to put down roots on the Senate side is much more a matter of personal taste than of strict status. As in the House, selection is by lottery in seniority order, but a senator might well prefer to retain a suite in the ornate and stately beaux arts Russell Building (the oldest) than to opt for a glass-enclosed, starkly functional office in the Hart Building (the newest). Indeed, some of the most senior senators, such as Kennedy, Hollings, and Moynihan, are located in the Russell Building while some of the newest senators are to be found in the Hart.

Colleagues and Other Strangers

Even the total membership of one's own party caucus in the House is too large a number of people to permit recognition of all of them by an individual. Outsiders sometimes marvel at the ability of the presiding officer of the House to call upon "the gentleman from Maryland" or "the gentlelady from Louisiana" with such apparent familiarity. In fact, certain members of the leadership staff who sit adjacent to the chair of the presiding officer are trained "member spotters" who whisper the relevant identifications to the chair.

The size of the House membership coupled with the shorter

term and a fairly large number of voluntary departures or
deaths in any given Congress produce a more changeable cast
of characters. But even a House member whom an outsider
would assume to be an intimate or at least a nodding acquaint-
ance of another representative can often turn out to be a
stranger. Sometimes an incident will illuminate for a House
member the surprisingly distant relationships that can prevail
in so large a body. An entry in the journal of a former House
member portrays such a moment:

Back in Washington this evening, I learned that John C. Watts, a
Democrat from Kentucky, had died of a heart attack. I remembered
reading in the paper last week a small piece that pointed out that he
was second-ranking Democrat on the Ways and Means Committee.
Had Wilbur Mills left the Congress, Watts would have been chairman
of that committee.

What struck me was the fact that I did not know John Watts. In
almost five years here, I never had the occasion to meet or speak to
him. Nor—until last week—had I read one line about him in print or
heard anyone mention his name. A man can come here and serve
many years. He can be very close to a position of real power, and at
the same time, be virtually anonymous.[10]

One should never be surprised when even those House
members with reason to know all of their party members draw
a blank on one of them. I was standing one day at the corner
of New Jersey and Constitution avenues talking to a member
of the House leadership when a fellow Democrat from a neigh-
boring state walked by. The congressman chatted with us but
as the conversation progressed, it became clear to me that the
leader had no idea whom we were talking to. After the member
left, the leader turned to me and said, "Who was that?" I
replied, "That's X from the state of Y." "Oh," the leader said,
"so that's X. I'd heard his name but can't honestly say I ever
laid eyes on him."

While it is not the case that every senator is familiar with
every other senator, the opportunity to interact with a larger

percentage of the membership is an advantage that senators enjoy and it contributes to the distinctive nature of the Senate.

In the Senate personal interaction among members is more important than it is in the House. Senators need to take the measure of a colleague as a person. The considerable personal influence of the individual senators and the ability that a single senator has to influence the legislative process make knowing what makes a colleague tick immensely important.

The Glittering Generalists and the Reluctant Specialists: Congress in Committee

In terms of the legislative process that begins with the introduction of bills and culminates in their enactment, the roles of House and Senate committees are identical. Both represent the division of labor that enables institutions responsible for lawmaking and oversight in diverse areas of public policy to parcel out manageable portions of it to smaller groups. Both groups specialize and develop expertise in particular areas. Both hold hearings, write legislation, advocate the passage of bills, and oversee their operation once they are law.

In terms of what meaning these committees have to individual senators or House members, there are substantial differences. Richard Fenno noted:

Senate committees are important as arenas in which decisions are made. But they are not especially important as sources of individual member influence—not when compared to House committees. That is, a Senator's committee membership adds far less to his total potential for influence inside his chamber than a Representative's committee membership adds to his potential for influence in his chamber.[11]

Fenno's point is that the House member is more a creature of his committee assignment than is the senator. The life-and-death nature of committee-assignment decisions in the House has no parallel in the Senate. House members' identities are

wrapped up in their committees because these committees provide them with their platform, their ability to amplify their
voices, their campaign contributions, and almost their very
identity. For a House member to be assigned to one of the
"exclusive" committees (Ways and Means, Appropriations,
Rules) that are considered so influential that service on another
committee is prohibited is a towering accomplishment; a seat
on the House Energy and Commerce Committee ensures a
generous supply of campaign money from corporate political
action committees (PACs) because of the panel's broad jurisdiction. By way of contrast, a senator will almost certainly get a
seat on one of the four choicest committees in his chamber:
Appropriations, Armed Forces, Finance, and Foreign Relations. And it does not end there for senators. They will also
serve on three or four other major committees because the
Senate has fewer people to cover the same policy turf as the
House. House members receive a slender slice of public policy
and, in devouring it, get to know every nut and raisin in the
filling. Senators get multiple helpings from several pies, but they
are not always certain whether it is lemon meringue or mince-
meat that they are eating at any given time.

While the number of House committees is not much larger
than the number of Senate committees, Senate committees have
fewer members. House Appropriations has almost sixty members; its Senate counterpart, which is the Senate's largest, has
only twenty-eight. Senate committees, typically, have fewer
than twenty members. The only House committees with twenty
or fewer members are the two committees that members struggle to avoid—House Administration and District of Columbia.
House Administration deals with internal housekeeping matters such as office space and parking; District of Columbia has
jurisdiction over the affairs of Washington, D.C., a city with no
voting power in Congress.

The individual senator looms even larger in the committee
setting than in the chamber as a whole, and of the fourteen
senators interviewed only one declined to cite committee dif-

ferences as a major distinction between the two chambers. William Hathaway, a Maine Democrat who had served four terms in the House before coming to the Senate, cited his frustration with the House committee system as a reason for deciding to run for the Senate. His comments reflect an earlier period before reforms in the House provided wider access to subcommittee chairmanships, but his reflections on size continue to hold true.

You have to be there a long time to get anywhere. If I had stayed there only now would I have made it. I would now be Chairman of the House Merchant Marine and Fisheries Committee. But even that is more by accident than anything else. Joe Karth, who was ahead of me, had a heart attack and quit. Jack Murphy got in trouble and went to jail. It's better now than it would have been because of the reforms. I would have been a subcommittee chairman at least, but in my first few years in the Senate I ended up heading four or five subcommittees.

The smaller size of the Senate committees promotes a faster track to leadership of the committee in a system where seniority is the rule but where greater influence is also given to very junior senators. Former senator Culver recalls the dramatic transition:

One of the great shocks when I arrived in the Senate was that instead of being on a committee with forty members or whatever, you're suddenly on a subcommittee where you may be one of two people who show up and if you've got a couple of proxies [votes you can cast on behalf of absent senators] there's nothing you can't get passed. It's like taking candy from a baby in terms of the opportunities that there are to effectively influence and shape the course of a bill in committee.

The size difference and the overall contrast in the role of Senate and House committees were underscored with great directness by Senator Phil Gramm, a Texas Republican who served two terms in the House as a Democrat and one as a Republican.

I have been a little bit surprised at the Senate in that the committees are less important over here. First of all, subcommittees are almost meaningless over here. The committees are small enough that all the work is done in full committee. And a subcommittee chairmanship is of relatively little value.

And quite frankly, Senate committees don't do a whole lot. At least not in my two years here. Much of the work is done on the floor.

While no other senator minimized the role of the Senate committee quite to the extent of Senator Gramm, all agreed that the committees just loom less large in the calculations of senators than of House members. This was discerned by congressional scholars Steven Smith and Christopher Deering, who noted that the objectives of senators in choosing one committee assignment over another are simply less differentiated than those of House members. While members tend to select the committee they want to serve on in terms of a number of calculations—such as whether or not the committee helps them gain reelection, rise in the House leadership, or shape policy—senators' decision rules seem less clear cut. Whatever the senators' ultimate goals, publicity for their committee work seems to be a more dominant factor in what committee they choose than it is with House members.[12]

THE LIMITS OF EXPERTISE FOR HOUSE MEMBERS

Being assigned to three major committees may cause senators to be spread very thin and denies them the opportunity that House members have to develop expertise in a single policy area. But few senators seem to think very highly of expertise—particularly if it is purchased at the price of being limited in what subjects they can speak out on. Multiple committee assignments are seen by senators as a kind of roving commission to speak authoritatively on a broad range of questions. What is particularly galling to House members is that they may have toiled on their subcommittee to build up expertise on an issue only to find that a senator has swooped down, seized the same issue, and is basking in the publicity to which the member thought his expertise entitled him.

New Jersey Democratic representative James Florio had established for himself a solid reputation as an expert on toxic waste by reason of his important role in the establishment of the Superfund, a program that makes financial assessments against chemical companies and other producers of toxic materials for the cleanup of polluted soil and water. He was also a major figure in efforts to rewrite the Superfund legislation—a man described as a "force to be reckoned with" by those responsible for the operation of the fund.[13]

But Florio, who is no laggard in getting the attention of the media, was known to have expressed frustration when New Jersey's junior senator, Frank Lautenberg, seized on the toxic-waste issue and the press turned increasingly to the senator and his activities in the field. Former senator John Culver saw this eclipsing of House members by senators as a general pattern that was demoralizing to the representatives.

The House members resent the fact, understandably, that they can work very hard in a public policy area and become genuine experts because of their association with their committee and its work and their forced concentration in the problem area, and yet the television news will be full of a senator who had been on the committee for a week and he's already a subcommittee chairman and he won't know one end from the other about the problem, but he's the one who will be quoted.

There he'll be popping off, and here is this highly informed, sophisticated, effective, eager House member who's going to die with the secret that he's the real expert. So it's not surprising that there's a lot of resentment.

UNDER THE DOME: HOUSE-SENATE CONFERENCES AND WHO WINS THEM

If senators are better situated to win the battle of publicity and visibility, one might expect that House members would shine in those situations where substantive and concentrated expertise might show. The conference committee to reconcile differences over House and Senate versions of the same bill would seem to be one such example where the House would consistently prevail. Seeing House members and senators in such close engagement might even reinforce the vision that the House gets its revenge in both substance and style. In fact, attempts to get a clear-cut idea of who wins in conference, that is, whose version of the bill is more likely to resemble the one signed by the president, have not been notably decisive.

The research over the past four decades as to who wins most often in conference ends up in an unsatisfying welter of qualifications, quibbles over what the word "win" means, and the ultimate retreat from a categorical answer: "It depends upon the circumstances."

Gilbert Steiner, in 1951, was the first to try to detect a pattern of House or Senate dominance in conference.[14] Steiner found a clear pattern of House dominance, especially in the areas of taxes, appropriations, and agricultural legislation.

Fifteen years later, Richard Fenno found that the Senate versions of bills in conference were the ones more often adopted because the Senate conferees (those chosen to represent the Senate in conferences) enjoyed greater support from the membership as a whole than did House members. Because of the decision-making structure of the Senate that emphasizes bipartisan consensus and House decisions which are frequently a reflection of the will of the dominant party, Senate conferees "not only represent the Senate—they are the Senate."[15]

But at the same time that the consensus seemed to be building on Senate dominance, John Manley put the case that the Senate's preeminence in conference was not so clear cut. He found that in conferences between the House Ways and Means Committee and the Senate Finance Committee, House conferees seemed more influential in the final outcome of Social Security bills while senators seemed more influential on trade and revenue issues.[16]

Somewhat later another investigator came to a general conclusion that the Senate tended to prevail in conference. His figure, that about 65 percent of items in disagreement were resolved according to the Senate position, is remarkably close to that of Fenno.[17]

Why is the Senate so consistently the winner on disputed conference items? A pair of researchers attempted to answer this question and came up with the conclusion that the Senate wins because, on money bills at least, it gets the bill after the House. The constitutional requirement that the House originate tax bills and the convention that appropriations also begin in the House make the Senate the court of last resort. The Senate becomes the place where lobbyists who did not get what they wanted in the House can turn their political firepower. Even House members look to the Senate to preserve amendments that they have included. The two scholars make two additional points: (1) When the Senate is the chamber initiating the action, the House tends to prevail more often; (2) there is nothing inherently superior to the Senate's rules or procedures that translates into victory—it merely seems to be the case that the last-acting chamber becomes the focus of more outside support whether that chamber be the House or the Senate. What may be the ultimate vindication of the reluctant specialists in the House is that most of what is acted upon in general by both houses originates in the House.[18]

SENATORS' PERCEPTIONS OF CONFERENCE VICTORS

While the bulk of the scholarly literature points with some consistency to the Senate as the victor in conferences, senators themselves do not think so. Why do senators think that the House positions usually prevail over that of their own chamber? The answer has to do with the manner in which conferees are selected by the leadership to represent their respective houses in conference. Both senators and House members are usually chosen as conferees because they serve on the committee that had jurisdiction over the bill. They attended the hearings and helped write the committee report that urged its passage by the entire chamber. That committee, however, is likely to be the only one the House conferee serves on. Senators, with broader

committee responsibilities, will serve on several panels and
hence be unable to devote themselves as single-mindedly to the
details of the bill as the more focused House members. This
perception of greater expertise on the part of House conferees
was uniform through the group of fourteen senators interviewed.

Senator Max S. Baucus, a Montana Democrat who spent
two terms in the House, said categorically, "The senators are
a lot less prepared than House members. They're spread thinner. And the consequence, in my judgment, is that House members tend to prevail in conference. When I'm at conference, I
try to exercise every advantage I have to keep up with the
House members because I am spread thin and have to rely
much more on my staff." Baucus's position was given qualified
support by a former senator, James Abourezk, who spent a
term in the House as a South Dakota Democrat before coming
to the Senate in 1973. "They know what they're doing, the
House members. They always knew more than I did on every
issue except one. Indians. I always felt I knew more about
Indians than they did."

House members, for their part, believe the myth of their
dominance. It seems to assuage the hurt of being considered so
much less majestic than the Senate in other realms. Senator
Richard S. Schweiker, a Pennsylvania Republican who spent
four terms in the House before going on to the Senate and later
serving in the Reagan Cabinet, recalled the malicious delight of
House members in flaunting their mastery of the details in
conference:

House guys have fewer committee responsibilities and know more of
the substance on a particular subject. They make a fetish of one-
upping the senators and proving that they've done their homework.

Also, because he's got so many committee obligations, a senator
may be involved in two or three conferences at the same time, while
the chances are that a congressman will be on only one or two at the
most. So the House guy can sit there and methodically wait for the
right time to put something through the conference.

Another reason that senators, in the face of some persuasive evidence to the contrary, believe that the House usually prevails in conference may be the product of the *noblesse oblige* that grants to the House a small advantage. Senators may also not be conscious of how powerful they actually are. Even though the pattern of Senate dominance is not uniform, most senators interviewed expressed surprise that the record of Senate success in conference might even be close to a draw. It is probably one of the few areas in which senators underestimate their influence.

The Role of Rules

It is difficult to overemphasize how profoundly the role of rules of procedure differs between the House and Senate. While the House member who wins a seat in the Senate is obviously more familiar with the legislative process than, let us say, a former governor or someone who operated a business, there are still major adjustments to be made.[19] Sometimes an event takes place early in the Senate career of a former House member that opens his or her eyes dramatically to the new system of rules. Hugh Scott had such an experience when he first came to the Senate after sixteen years in the House.

One of the philosophical gurus of the Senate at the time I was elected was John Williams from Delaware. I paid a courtesy call on him since he was one person I particularly wanted guidance from.

He said to me, "What do you want to know?" And I said that I'd been over on the Senate floor but I'd never studied the Senate rules. I asked him what I needed to do if I wanted to make a speech. He said, "You stand up." And I said: "What do I do then?" And he said, "The presiding officer recognizes you."

So I told him that in the House, [Speaker] Sam Rayburn didn't have to recognize me unless he wanted to. So Williams said that it's not that way in the Senate. "They've got to recognize you because your power to do mischief is too great if they don't."

Well, I thought about what John Williams said about mischief and about a month later I went to talk to [Majority Whip] Mike

Mansfield. We didn't know each other very well and I said to him, "Senator, can I have a minute or two to talk on this bill?"

"Well," he replied, "I'm afraid you're too late. I don't think we have enough time left." So I said, "That's all right, I'll just ask for a quorum call, and that will take twice the amount of time I needed to say my piece."

So he said, "Well, I'll get you recognized," and he did it right away and from that time on we had the most cordial relationship.

By resorting to a rule that enables a senator to request a time-consuming quorum call, Scott was reminding Mansfield that it was better to comply with even an untimely or even unreasonable request than to risk tying up the Senate's business. If mischief making is what a senator wishes to pursue, the rules allow it. House rules do not confer this ability on members. As another former House member, John Culver, put it:

If you just want to be unpleasant and have a temper tantrum and if you just want to be excessively self-obsessed, you can have a field day in the Senate. You can break all the toys in the sandbox if that's what you want in order to get your way and you can pout with very great effect. You really can't do that the same way in the House. The rules of the Senate are congenial to permitting the least consequential member to shut the place down if he's smart enough or willful enough to do it. If you are one in a hundred, it really doesn't matter a lot how long you've been there. That gives any individual power—real power—in institutional terms. He just has to be dealt with.

RULES AND SIZE

Senate rules differ from House rules largely because the Senate is a quarter the size of the House. But beneath a Senate system of rules that magnifies the role of the individual senator and makes him or her so imposing there lurks the constitutional principle of equal representation for all states. The smallness of the Senate and its different basis of representation seem inextricably linked in historical terms. So whether the individual's prerogatives were magnified because he or she was part of a small body or represented a whole state rather than merely a portion of one is difficult to sort out.

At the turn of the twentieth century Senator Henry Cabot Lodge, a Massachusetts Republican (and grandfather and namesake of the 1960 Republican vice-presidential candidate), wrote a series of articles on the Senate for *Scribner's Magazine*. In these articles he made the case for the constitutional superiority of the Senate, asserting that

in the formation of the Senate the States were retaining for themselves all the powers they believed needful for their safety, and as everything was theirs to give or withhold, they were naturally liberal in their endowment of the body which was to continue to represent them under a system where they necessarily parted with so much.[20]

At the same time that Lodge was exalting the Senate as a repository of state sovereignty, he also made the case that smallness was the reason for the simplicity of the Senate's rules. Writing about the first meeting of the Senate, which took place in Federal Hall in New York in April 1789 without the senators from North Carolina and Rhode Island, Lodge noted:

These twenty-two gentlemen . . . sat together in one not very large room and talked matters over with an informality and familiarity which have never entirely departed from Senate debates. . . .

This small body of men, sitting in this way in private, with comparatively little to do and with no record of the proceedings but the journal, did not require anything very elaborate in the way of rules. Business was largely transacted by general assent, and with much regard for the convenience of each Senator, habits which have survived unchanged to the present time.[21]

Smallness was also stressed as the defining character of the Senate by Woodrow Wilson:

[The Senate] is small enough to make it safe to allow individual freedom to its members, and to have, at the same time, such order and sense of proportion in its proceedings as is characteristic of small bodies, like boards of college trustees or of commercial directors, who feel that their main object is business, not speechmaking, and so say all that is necessary without being tedious, and do what they are called upon to do without need of driving themselves with hurrying rules. Such rules, they seem to feel, are meant only for big assemblies which have no power of self-control.[22]

The rules of procedure that are promoted by the Senate's smallness magnify the influence of the individual by allowing a single senator to intervene—often decisively—in the legislative process. Power of this magnitude is accorded to only a handful of the top leaders in the House. This power when multiplied by 100 produces an institution far less predictable than the House.

What are these rules of procedure in the Senate that repose such great power in the hands of individuals? What gives them "the power to do mischief" or "to break all the toys in the sandbox"? And how do these powers differ from those available to House members? The two mentioned most frequently by the fourteen senators were extended debate and the absence of a general rule of germaneness.

EXTENDED DEBATE

Extended debate by a senator or group of senators, which in its most extreme form is known as the filibuster, is one of the most distinctive features of the Senate. Those intimately familiar with House rules find it hard to adjust to. Parliamentarian of the Senate, Floyd A. Riddick, whose career had begun as an expert on House rules, found extended debate a major adjustment when moving from the House. This was apparent in a 1979 interview with Associate Senate Historian Donald A. Ritchie.

After I got to the Senate I had to try to forget all of the rules of the House because their rules are so different. The biggest contrast I'd say is unlimited debate in the Senate as contrasted to very limited debate in the House. And the use of the previous question in the House as contrasted to no limit on debate in the Senate.

Ritchie commented, "I suppose with the size of the House there's almost no other way they could operate." Riddick replied, "I think that's true, I think it's a problem of numbers."[23]

The history of extended debate in the Senate can be traced to a revision of the Senate rules that took place in 1806 after the Senate had been in operation for seventeen years. Until that rules revision, Senate Rule 8 allowed debate to be terminated by the calling for a vote on "the previous question." Such a motion was privileged: It could be moved and seconded at any time and if passed by a majority vote debate would be terminated. That provision for closing debate was dropped in 1806, and between that date and 1917 there was no way to terminate debate in the Senate. Just a few years after the Senate instituted unlimited debate the House limited it by adopting the previous question rule. In 1811, the House made the motion for previous question nondebatable, thus precipitating an immediate vote on whatever matter of business is pending.[24]

What caused the Senate to institute *cloture,* or limitation on debate, in 1917 was the inability of the Senate to vote on the armed-ship bill that had been favored by the Woodrow Wilson administration to protect U.S. merchant vessels from German submarines. Wilson used his constitutional authority to call a special session of the Senate. On March 8, 1917, the Senate adopted Rule 22 permitting a vote on cloture on the petition of sixteen senators. If two-thirds of the senators present and voting approved the termination of debate, cloture would be invoked. In 1975 Rule 22 was modified to allow cloture if supported by three-fifths of the entire membership (sixty senators).[25]

The history of closing off debate in the Senate has progressed from impossible (1806–1917) to almost impossible (1917–1975) to very difficult (1975–present).

But while the standards for cutting off debate have been eased, that is a far cry from saying that debate can be cut off readily. For example, even after cloture is voted, each of the 100 senators is still allowed one hour of debate and time-consuming

amendments can still be offered. This led Senator Phil Gramm
to conclude that the principle of extended debate stands virtually intact:

The rules of the Senate give tremendous power to the individual
member if he feels strongly about something. He can literally stop the
Senate. For example, in my two years in the Senate, we have never
had a debate stopped. If an individual wanted to debate and wanted
to prevent a vote from occurring, we have never in my experience
taken action that stopped him. We had cloture motions adopted, but
after cloture you've got 100 hours of debate. So if that one member
really is opposed to something and is willing to stand up on the issue,
it is very, very difficult to do anything.

Late in a congressional session when the Senate faces adjournment and time is running out to pass critical bills that
must pass in order for the government to remain in operation,
the filibuster (or even the threat of it) can be used to devastating
effect as the Senate can conduct no other business on the floor
so long as the debate continues.

This almost unlimited ability to block the Senate's schedule
and the feeble claims of the House members to debate time
summed up for former senator and House member Richard
Schweiker the differences between the two bodies:

I was one of the real experts in the House on the all-volunteer army
and the debate for the renewal of the draft came up in the House. But
the most I could get was five minutes of speaking time in the House
debates on that issue.

I got to the Senate and I was able to introduce an amendment even
though the chairman of the Armed Services Committee was very
much against the idea. So here I was a freshman Republican and even
though I'd lost in committee I kept my pride and went to the floor
and beat the chairman. So there it was: I'd gone from the House,
barely able to speak three minutes on a major issue, to upsetting the
chairman by making a case for it on the floor.

What enabled this senator to pull off such a feat was the
unlimited debate in his new chamber. But there is another form

of flexibility that works to the benefit of senators: the absence of a germaneness rule such as the one that prevails in the House.

THE GERMANENESS QUESTION

The absence of a general germaneness rule in the Senate was pointed to by most of the senators interviewed as the procedural difference between the House and Senate that most enhanced the power of senators. Put simply, the House rules require that amendments to a bill made on the floor must be germane, that is, relevant and pertinent, to the bill itself. With certain exceptions, senators can introduce floor amendments that have nothing at all to do with the bill as it comes to the floor from a committee.

The fact that the Senate lacks a germaneness rule and the House has one reflects the difference between the two houses in the importance of committees. What the germaneness rule in the House really says is that, as a rule, the work of the committee shall not be tampered with on the floor. If a House committee has duly reported out a bill and its structure and substance have been approved by the Rules Committee (a stop that Senate bills do not have to make) there is a strong resistance to any amendment offered on the floor, particularly if it comes from someone who is not a member of the bill-writing committee.

There is no better example of the enormous policymaking power vested in senators because they do not have to conform to the strictures of a germaneness rule than the Gramm-Rudman-Hollings Act of 1986. This radical approach to reducing the federal budget was offered as a nongermane amendment to a bill extending the federal debt limit. The principal author of the amendment, Senator Phil Gramm, reflected upon what he did and what he would have been unable to do as a House member.

In the House I would never have had the opportunity to offer Gramm-Rudman. I had to have a [legislative] vehicle that *had* to be adopted. The House rules are such that any change in the Budget Act had to go

not to the Budget Committee but to the Rules Committee. The
Speaker appoints the Rules Committee and there is no way in the
world you're going to strengthen the budget process or impose any
binding constraints through the committee process in the House.

So I had started really working on this idea that became Gramm-
Rudman in 1982 when I was in the House. And when I got to the
Senate I saw the vehicle I had been waiting for—the two trillion dollar
debt ceiling. So I offered the Gramm-Rudman-Hollings law as an
amendment to the debt ceiling extension, a bill that *has* to be passed
on a timely basis for the government to continue to function.

Now I just could not have done that in the House. Because they
would have ruled my amendment nongermane. In fact they would
have ruled any amendment to the debt ceiling nongermane except
maybe changing the numbers.

The implications of the germaneness differences go well
beyond the substance of policy—they involve the political dynamics of the two bodies and the ability of senators and members to wound one another politically.

Because they are able to introduce amendments on the floor
virtually at will, any senator can demand a recorded vote of his
colleagues at almost any time. Going on record, particularly on
controversial issues, is an act that most politicians would prefer
to avoid.

A lobbyist for a major civil rights organization put the
punitive aspects of the lack of germaneness requirements this
way:

If a troublemaker like [Senator] Jesse Helms [R-N.C.] a month before
the congressional elections wants a recorded vote on a school prayer,
or a busing, or an abortion amendment, he can get it in most instances.
At the very least, he can get a tabling motion which is a procedural
vote, but understandably can be sold as a substantive vote also. It is
much easier in the Senate to get a recorded vote and force someone
to take a position.

Bert Carp, who is currently vice-president of Turner Broadcasting and the individual in charge of lobbying for that cable

network, notes the same destructive power but observes that it
is used sparingly.

Senators don't like to vote on controversial matters; they end up
disappointing large numbers of people. It's this power to wound one
another and to cause havoc. That's what causes it to be used so
cautiously. But the institution does not lean so much on binding rules
as it does on conventions of courtesy.

So while it is true that the sheer difference in volume between House rules and Senate rules (eleven volumes of House
rules and precedents versus a single volume plus ninety pages
for Senate rules and precedents) is emblematic of the differences
in complexity of procedure, the greatest differences are informal. Even if the Senate had a substantially larger body of
regulations, the smallness of the Senate would permit the development of understandings among senators on a face-to-face
basis that would not be possible for the larger House. What may
exemplify best the difference between the formal and canonical
House and the informal and subjective Senate is the phenomenon of the *unanimous consent agreement.*

While employed in both chambers to dispose of routine or
noncontroversial business, the unanimous consent agreement in
the Senate is an informal device that specifies the rules of debate
on virtually every bill. The House requires the Rules Committee to issue a rule or special order after a bill leaves committee
but before it reaches the floor as to what extent a bill can be
amended and how much debate time will be accorded propo-
nents and foes of the bill. The House version of the procedure
is the subject of formal, public hearings by the Rules Committee; the Senate's version is formed by informal arrangements
between party leaders. In the House, it is not even authentically
unanimous because it is adopted by majority vote; in the Senate,
every last senator must agree on the terms and conditions of the
debate and vote.[26]

On the face of it, procedures which grant so much discretion to the individual would seem to promote an individualism so excessive that timely action would be virtually impossible. Indeed, where interests conflict, as they so often do in the Senate, the requirement for unanimity or near-unanimity on many matters has been seen as a prescription for anarchy. Senator Warren Rudman (R-N.H.), a man with a reputation for thoughtfulness, describes senators as "independent contractors" in their assertion of individual prerogatives and says, "We've got so many checks and balances around here, we're frozen." Then, he warns, "Either we make major changes or the House will become the dominant body."[27] The free rein given to individuals in the Senate also came under attack from political scientist Norman Ornstein, who complained, "It doesn't just bend over backwards to protect the intense feelings of its minorities, it lets individuals run roughshod over any semblance of institutional process."[28] The Senate has come under fire for allowing rules designed to protect minority interests to become subverted and used as devices for obstructionism and personal pique.

No one familiar with the Senate can doubt that such abuses are widespread. And one does not get very far into a discussion with a senator or staff person about Senate rules without hearing the names of Senator Jesse Helms (R-N.C.) and Senator Howard Metzenbaum (D-Ohio) as people who carry individualism too far. One senator observed, "The rules around here are such that one determined member can wreak havoc with the schedule; even members who are generally disliked and who are notorious for being obnoxious and abusive, but people don't often call their hand because it's better to tolerate them than to screw around with the rules. You don't stir things up just to get at a Jesse Helms." Hearing his delaying tactics on the floor of the Senate described as "monkey-wrench politics"—a willingness to "throw a monkey wrench into the works no matter what happens"—Senator Metzenbaum had a quick reply: "You say monkey wrench and that's bad. You say obstructionist and that's bad. You say public interest and that's good."[29]

It would appear at first glance that obstructionism and the public interest are totally incompatible, and that Senator Metzenbaum's attempt to liken them is self-serving. But dismissing the hyperindividualism of the Senate as no more than a symptom of the fragmentation of American democracy would be a mistake. It would likewise be inappropriate to conclude that the absence of such strong checks on the will of the majority in the House necessarily promotes the public interest. It is more useful to see the operations of the two houses as promoting different kinds of democracy, both of which are essential. Consider the two models of democracy that have been referred to as "adversary democracy" and "unitary democracy."[30] Adversary democracy as it pertains to Congress refers to the faithful representation of the various interests of their states and districts by senators and House members and the practice of bargaining among members for benefits and protections for those constituencies. Unitary democracy, in contrast, involves the establishment of a consensus among legislators on what is the common or national interest.

The American legislative system is based on geographical representation and no member of Congress is elected by the nation as a whole. Only the voters in the 50 states or the 435 congressional districts have any direct control over the composition of Congress. With the fate of all senators and representatives in the hands of voters in these smaller geographical units, adversary democracy enjoys a built-in advantage in both chambers. Indeed, much legislation bears the unmistakable seams of having been assembled out of 535 components; it reflects a distributive strategy in which policy is subordinated to parochial considerations. Increasingly, moreover, American elections turn not on the major issues of the day but upon the sole question of who can deliver the best set of particularized benefits to a state or district. Adversary values clearly dominate the world of congressional elections.

Senators and House members come to Washington to look after the interests of the citizens who elected them, and who, indeed, would advocate and defend those local interests if not those very legislators? But they are also United States senators and United States representatives. The laws they make are binding on all Americans, not just on the voters who sent them to Washington. If the national interest could be defined as no more than the sum of all of the local interests represented by the 535 congressional members, then the adversary model would be the only one with which we need concern ourselves. It is certainly possible to imagine a system of government whose resources were so abundant that it could literally give every interest what it wanted and, indeed, there have been times in the American past when it seemed that we verged on such a system. But even if resources can be distributed equally to all claimants, values cannot.

The framers of the Constitution, for all of their belief in the beneficial interplay of interests, believed that the whole was larger than merely the sum of its parts. James Madison expressed his concern over what he called "the national character" and defended the inclusion of a Senate in the Constitution as a more reliable expression of that character than the House.

Madison wrote, in #63 of the *Federalist,* that national character "can never be sufficiently possessed by a numerous and changeable body. It can only be found in a number so small, that a sensible degree of the praise and blame of public measures may be the portion of each individual; or in an assembly so durably invested with public trust, that the pride and consequences of its members may be sensibly incorporated with the reputation and prosperity of the community."

Madison seemed to be making a case for the "unitary quality" of the Senate, saying, in effect, that its continuity made it a more national institution than the House. In a later passage in *Federalist* #63, Madison refers to the "cool and deliberate sense of community" in free governments that sometimes gives way to "irregular passions" and "temporary errors and delusions" on the part of the people. He stresses the need for a "temperate and respectable body of citizens" to intervene to quell the passions until "reason, justice, and truth can regain their authority over the public mind."

Representatives, with their proximity to the people by reason of their direct election and with their greater responsiveness by reason of their two-year term, were expected to resonate to popular passions. As Madison wrote in *Federalist* #52, the House would have "an immediate dependence on, and intimate sympathy with, the people." This presupposed an adversary role; House members were to give voice to the concerns of their constituents in unmodulated volume. To do otherwise would be to impede the free interplay of interests that was at the heart of the constitutional design. The House was to be the arena of sentiments that were not only passionate but the products of numerically small and specialized segments of the population.

But can the considerable prerogatives of senators and a set of rules that promotes great individualism serve the public interest? At first glance it might seem unlikely that the values of unitary democracy could be promoted by a system of rules that provides so many opportunities for blockage and obstruction. But George Reedy notes, "The Senate does *not* prevent the majority from ruling; it merely prevents the majority from doing everything it wants to do when it wants to do it. The Senate does not grant the minority the right to rule. It merely grants the minority the right to block legislation until it has been demonstrated that there is a clearcut, consistent majority behind it and until it is apparent that the minority is willing to remain within the community when it is forced to give in to legislation that it considers abhorrent."[31]

Indeed, Mansbridge has observed that protection and group unity are not always at odds, for the individual protection afforded by the veto can sometimes reinforce group unity.[32] This may be particularly applicable to small face-to-face groups

like the Senate. While it is certainly true that political conflict
based on the defense of parochial interests is a major force in
the Senate, the simple compactness and the face-to-face quality
of senatorial interaction may have the effect of muting and
attenuating conflict. And, "while face-to-face contact is not
logically related to the discovery of a common interest and can
sometimes intensify conflict, it usually seems to encourage participants to find solutions they can all support."[33]

The framers of the Constitution created a Senate in which
all states would have equal voice so that the rights of the
smallest and least populous states would be protected. The
smallness of the Senate as a body and the rules that grew out
of that compactness accentuate those protections of minority
opinion, but they may also promote consensus by the simple
fact that senators are likely to get to know one another and so
take the measure of colleagues as individuals. "Face-to-face
contact," Mansbridge writes, "works best for the unitary end
of cementing friendship." She adds that "mutual knowledge
and subtle communication make fuller empathy possible so that
each member can more easily make the other's interest his or
her own."[34]

But does the Senate qualify as a face-to-face body? One
condition that has been laid down as a standard is that everyone
in the body knows everyone else in it.[35]

The average senator, as I have already noted, does not know
every last colleague, but there is evidence that senators know
and interact with a higher percentage of colleagues than do
House members. Michael Foley found that difference in committee size and the number of individual committee assignments between the House and the Senate resulted in the typical
House member knowing about 11 percent of his or her colleagues and the average senator about one-third of the total
membership of the Senate.[36]

The degree of personal intimacy in a circle of House friends
is likely to be greater than that among senators with their more
glancing contacts and the greater presence of staff as intermedi-

aries. In the aggregate, however, the senator is able to take the
personal measure of more of his or her colleagues. Such associations have a great impact on the institution at large. Networks
of personal association in the Senate come closer to being insti-
tutionwide than in the House. Such networks, moreover, are
less specialized by subject area or geography. Friendship of a
kind peculiar to the Senate influences profoundly the way the
Senate operates. Former senator Richard S. Schweiker, a Pennsylvania Republican, described the importance of personal relations in the Senate.

In the Senate reason prevails more, logic prevails more, and personal
and close friendships are more important than they are in the House
because there's no place to hide in the Senate. If you had a difference
of opinion between House members of different parties, it very seldom
got resolved or adjudicated in any way. It was just an accepted fact
of life.
    But if you clashed on the Senate floor, heatedly, with somebody,
chances are that one or the other would make an effort by the end of
the day to be congenial and converse and interact with that person,
knowing that he differed. You sort of went out of your way after
clashing with somebody to go over and say hello, shake his hand, wish
him well.

Much of the rancor in debate in the contemporary House
is a reflection of the desperation of the Republicans because of
the apparent permanency of their status as the minority party.
Their frustration expresses itself in sniping at the Democratic
leadership with a sustained ferocity that is unknown in the
Senate, where partisan control has shifted more readily. But the
structure of the House intensifies this conflict. Administering a
tongue-lashing to a colleague and then withdrawing into the
recesses of a large and segmented membership seems more
typical of the House than of the Senate. Making amends for
acrimonious comments made in debate seems more characteristic of the Senate than the House.
    Take the case of the filibustering of a military authorization

bill by Senator John W. Warner (R-Va.) at the time of the Iraqi
attack on the frigate U.S.S. *Stark* in the Persian Gulf. Warner
was challenged on the floor by Senator Daniel Patrick Moynihan, who implied in his remarks that that was a poor time to
be filibustering against a bill to aid the navy. Moynihan's implication precipitated a heated exchange and Moynihan stalked off
the floor. Shortly thereafter, however, Warner showed up in the
Senate dining room bearing a gift bottle of Irish whiskey for
Moynihan with an invitation to share the contents.[37]

It is worth noting that Warner's gift to Moynihan was a
gesture that reached across party lines. One product of the
intimacy and face-to-face nature of the Senate is that partisanship expresses itself differently than in the House.

NOTES

1. U.S. Congress, House, *The Capitol,* 93rd Congress, 1st Session, 1973, p. 11.
2. *New York Times,* Monday, December 1, 1986.
3. Steven V. Roberts, "Pick a Seat, (but not) Any Seat," *New York Times,* Monday,
   December 1, 1986.
4. Ibid.
5. Roberts, op. cit.; Ross K. Baker, *Friend and Foe in the U.S. Senate* (New York: The
   Free Press, 1980), p. 95; and U.S. Congress, House, *The Capitol,* 96th Congress, 2d
   Session, 1981, p. 97.
6. Roberts, op. cit.
7. Baker, op. cit., p. 96.
8. *New York Times,* Wednesday, December 10, 1986.
9. Ibid.
10. Donald Riegle (with Trevor Armbrister), *O Congress* (Garden City, N.Y.: Double-
    day, 1972), p. 147.
11. Richard F. Fenno, Jr., *Congressmen in Committee* (Boston: Little, Brown, 1973),
    p. 147.
12. Steven S. Smith and Christopher J. Deering, *Committee in Congress* (Washington,
    D.C.: Congressional Quarterly Press, 1984), pp. 111–112. See also Richard F.
    Fenno, Jr., *Congressmen in Committee.*
13. Michael Barone and Grant Ujifusa, *The Almanac of American Politics, 1988*
    (Washington, D.C.: National Journal, 1988), p. 738.
14. Gilbert Y. Steiner, *The Congressional Conference Committee, Seventieth to Eighti-
    eth Congresses* (Urbana, Ill.: University of Illinois Press, 1951).
15. Richard F. Fenno, Jr., *The Power of the Purse* (Boston: Little Brown, 1966), and
    David Vogler, "Patterns of Dominance on Conference Committees," *Midwest
    Journal of Political Science,* 14 (1970), pp. 303–320.
16. John Manley, *The Politics of Finance* (Boston: Little, Brown, 1970).
17. John Ferejohn, "Who Wins in Conference Committee?" *Journal of Politics,* 27
    (November 1975), pp. 1033–1046.

18. Gerald S. Strom and Barry S. Rundquist, "A Revised Theory of Winning in House-Senate Conferences," *American Political Science Review,* 71 (June 1977), pp. 448–453.
19. Richard F. Fenno, Jr., "Adjusting to the U.S. Senate," unpublished paper, photocopy, p. 16.
20. Henry Cabot Lodge, "The Senate," *Scribner's Magazine,* 34 (1903), p. 542.
21. Lodge, op. cit., p. 545.
22. Woodrow Wilson, *Congressional Government* (Boston: Houghton-Mifflin, 1885), pp. 216–217.
23. Senate Historical Office, *Oral History Interview with Floyd A. Riddick,* conducted by Donald A. Ritchie, Washington, D.C., June 26, 1978–February 15, 1979, pp. 16–17.
24. Malcolm E. Jewell and Samuel C. Patterson, *The Legislative Process in the United States,* 4th ed. (New York: Random House, 1986), pp. 102–103.
25. Walter J. Oleszek, *Congressional Procedures and the Policy Process,* 2d ed. (Washington, D.C.: CQ Press, 1984), p. 188.
26. Oleszek, *Congressional Procedures,* pp. 156–159.
27. Martin Tolchin, "Senate Deplores Disarray in New Chamber of Equals," *New York Times,* Sunday, November 24, 1984.
28. Quoted in Helen Dewar, "Senate Faces Institutional Identity Crisis," *Washington Post,* Monday, November 26, 1984.
29. Steven V. Roberts, "Senate's New Breed Shuns Novice Role," *New York Times,* Monday, November 26, 1984.
30. See Jane J. Mansbridge, *Beyond Adversary Democracy* (Chicago: University of Chicago Press, 1983), and David J. Vogler and Sidney R. Waldman, *Congress and Democracy* (Washington, D.C.: Congressional Quarterly, 1985).
31. George E. Reedy, *The U.S. Senate* (New York: Crown, 1986), p. 197.
32. Mansbridge, op. cit., p. 263.
33. Ibid., p. 271.
34. Ibid., pp. 270–271.
35. Peter Laslett, "The Face to Face Society," in Peter Laslett, ed., *Philosophy, Politics, and Society* (Oxford: Blackwell, 1956), p. 157.
36. Michael Foley, *The New Senate* (New Haven: Yale University Press, 1980), p. 172.
37. *New York Times,* Friday, May 22, 1987.

3

Raw Numbers and Concurrent
Majorities

Partisanship and Leadership in the Two Houses

REFLECTING ON HIS EXPERIENCE in the two chambers of
Congress, Senator Donald Riegle (D-Mich.) emphasized one distinction that he believed to be essential
in understanding the differences between the House and Senate.

I think that as a general proposition, the Senate is a less partisan place
than the House. That's probably due to the fact that it's a smaller body
and the personal relations are stronger and have a greater bearing and
that tends a lot of times to offset partisan differences.

I've noticed, for example, over here that when colleagues take
trips together the political differences disappear pretty fast. These
delegations are usually pretty small and when people share experi-
ences like going overseas together that's part of the specialness of the
Senate where you can build personal relationships either within or
across party lines. . . .

My experience in the House is that that center aisle marks a wider
division than is true in the Senate. I think that in the Senate [there is]
that greater opportunity for intimacy, members one with the other, on
committees, riding back and forth on the subway cars. All the other
things that tend to create personal contacts tend to soften the party
divisions.

The magnification of the individual and his prominence in
the legislative process tends to make the Senate a less partisan
place than the House. By one widely accepted standard—the
percentage of times a majority of Democrats votes against a

majority of Republicans—the House-Senate differences in partisanship are measurable. For example, in 1988, 47 percent of the roll-call votes in the House reflected a sharp partisan split while 42 percent of the Senate votes divided along party lines.[1]

During the late 1970s and early 1980s the Senate was only marginally more partisan than the House. But interviews with the fourteen senators suggest strongly that these ex–House members perceive the Senate to be a less partisan place and that it is in interpersonal relationships and informal arrangements that the contrasts appear. One setting common to both houses in which differences in partisanship express themselves with particular clarity is in committee.

Bicameral Differences in Committee Partisanship

Committee service tends to be a major factor in determining with whom a legislator interacts, along with membership in one's state delegation in the chamber. Committees meet in relatively small rooms, share staff, caucus together, mark up bills together, and represent the chamber on conference committees. It would be logical, then, that the more committee settings in which legislators find themselves, the more colleagues they will have the opportunity to get to know. Because senators serve on more committees than House members, their circles of associations are larger and encompass more of the membership. While friendship and intimacy may be more intense among the House colleagues thrown together on a 30-member committee in a 435-member House, senators serving on 3 committees of 10 members each might have an opportunity to establish personal ties with fully a third of their colleagues in a 100-member Senate.[2]

The Iran-Contra hearings of 1987 provide an excellent opportunity to compare a House committee and a Senate committee working side by side on the same issue and determine how partisanship figured on each side.

The hearings were conducted not by a single committee

consisting of House members and senators but by two separate committees meeting jointly to take testimony and file separate reports. Both were "select" committees; that is, they were created for a specific purpose and would disband after issuing their reports.

Different views of partisanship came into play at the very beginning of the process of investigating illegal arms sales to Iran and diversion of the profits of those sales to the Contra guerrilla forces attempting to overthrow the anti-American government of Nicaragua. When House and Senate leaders selected members for the committee, their criteria as to the partisan spirit of those selected could hardly have been more different.

In the House, both Republican and Democratic leaders chose members for the intensity of their partisanship. Republican leader Bob Michel passed up two senior representatives from New York who occasionally voted with the Democrats in favor of three younger Republicans, Jim Courter of New Jersey, Michael DeWine of Ohio, and Bill McCollum of Florida, who could defend staunchly the Republican president. In the Senate, however, both Democratic leader Robert C. Byrd and Republican leader Bob Dole chose senators known for their mild partisanship. Byrd, the majority leader, made the first selections, based on moderate partisanship. Dole was reported to have looked over Byrd's list and made his choices on the same basis.[3]

Republican senator Paul Trible of Virginia ascribed the relatively mild partisanship of the Senate to its small size, saying, "You have to work with this person today even if you disagree with him because you may need him tomorrow." Citing the rules that govern the smaller chamber, William S. Cohen (R-Maine), another member of the Senate Iran-Contra Committee, said, "One or two people can tie this place in knots." He added, "In the House they can ignore [Republicans], but things that don't have bipartisan support don't get done here."[4]

It is not simply size that governs the intensity of partisanship in the two houses but size combined with partisan balance. The Republicans are outnumbered in the House at this writing (the 1988 elections) by eighty-five seats—an almost insuperable barrier to control of the chamber given its modest turnover rate. Democrats outnumbered the Republicans in the Senate by only ten seats. So there is, then, a realistic possibility of the Republicans recapturing the Senate sometime in the future. When people think that the shoe may likely be on the other foot during their tenures, they behave differently than those who have no such expectations.

Senate committees in general are joint enterprises run by the chair and the ranking minority member. The minority party members on a Senate committee are authentic and influential players. The influence enjoyed by minority party members is a combination of the courtesy and consideration toward the individual in the small Senate; the other component is a frank recognition that a single alienated senator can cause havoc. While the treatment accorded minority members on the House side varies from committee to committee, nowhere is it as deferential as in the Senate. In virtually every instance they are, in the words of Senator Trible, "frankly irrelevant."[5]

The helplessness of minority members in the House—even those who serve on key committees—was summed up by Representative Bill Frenzel, a Minnesota Republican, who lamented the limited role played by Republicans on the powerful Ways and Means Committee during the drafting of the tax reform bill in the 100th Congress. Although he was fifth-ranking Republican on the committee, Frenzel was reported to have said that Republicans were "spectators mostly," largely ignored by Chairman Dan Rostenkowski.[6]

Some senators observed that the degree of partisanship on any committee, whether House or Senate, also depended on the nature of the subject matter and whether it tended to process legislation with strong ideological coloration or have within its jurisdiction policies that affected economic or professional interests. One senator recalled that the Senate Judiciary Committee, with its battles over abortion, was far more partisan than House Merchant Marine and Fisheries, where members of both parties from coastal districts worked harmoniously to foster fishing and shipping interests. All things being equal, however, the senators were unanimous that partisan acrimony was stronger on House committees and that high-ranking minority members on House committees were less influential.

Leaders and Followers in the House and Senate

When asked about the nature of modern leadership in the United States Senate, Connecticut Democrat Abraham Ribicoff once quipped that if he had ever taken a pencil from his pocket in the presence of Majority Leader Robert C. Byrd, he was certain that Byrd would have offered to sharpen it for him.

Byrd personifies what Barbara Sinclair has termed "service leadership."[7] While she applies the term to the leadership of the House, it is even more appropriate to the leadership of the Senate. Here again, size differences seem to account for House-Senate contrasts. Senator James Abourezk, a South Dakota Democrat, put the case bluntly:

There is a huge difference and it's only because there are so many House members. The leadership does not really have to pay attention to the individual members that the Senate leaders do.

Woodrow Wilson came very close to denying that formal leadership was even possible in the Senate. In 1885 he wrote:

The public now and again picks out here and there a Senator who seems to act and to speak with true instinct of statesmanship and who unmistakably merits the confidence of colleagues and of people. But such a man, however eminent, is never more than *a* Senator. No on is *the* Senator. No one may speak for his party as well as for himself; no one exercises the special trust of acknowledged leadership.[8]

While much has changed in the century since Wilson wrote, aside from a brief period in the late 1950s when Lyndon Johnson exercised a singular degree of control over the body, Wilson's observations are not wholly obsolete.

Differences have been noted as to the qualities most prevalent in House and Senate leaders. Neil MacNeil noted in the early 1960s that the Senate's greatest leaders have been its great orators, while the most eminent House leaders have been those who could persuade or force the House to act. Rarely, however, he noted, do these expressive and instrumental qualities exist in the same person. Significantly, he found them in Henry Clay, a man who began his legislative career in the Senate, switched to the House, where he was elected Speaker as a freshman in 1811, and finished his lawmaking career in the Senate.[9]

Senator Paul Sarbanes (D-Md.) dwelt on two differences between the House and Senate that affect leadership most profoundly: the House and Senate rules, and the ability of the House leadership to use the power of its majority. House leadership, according to Sarbanes, "has a superior ability to channel and focus things over what is available to Senate leadership." In regard to rules, Sarbanes emphasized the ability of individual senators to introduce amendments from the floor without needing to get the amendment approved by an arm of leadership. As for the power of 218 votes, the simple majority of the House, to be decisive, Sarbanes observed that both House and Senate leaders would prefer to cajole members into supporting them, because "it's probably a better way to lead." But if cajoling does not work, "the House leaders can just use the raw numbers to move the thing right along. In the Senate, one person, whether he's on the majority side or on the minority side, can keep leadership from moving the thing on through. You really have to say that in the Senate, leadership is in the hands of the membership."

The stark contrast between leadership in the House and Senate becomes even more vivid when one broadens the definition of leadership to include not only the top party and institutional leaders (Speaker of the House and floor leaders in the House and Senate) but committee chairs as well. Virtually every senator is either chairman of a committee or subcommittee or ranking minority member on one or the other. If leadership is so defined, every senator is a leader. This has been true for some time.

Robert Peabody noted that in the 93rd Congress (1973–1974) only one senator—Republican William V. Roth, Jr., of Delaware—did not hold at least one ranking minority position on either of his committees. That leadership resources were spread so evenly in the Senate led Peabody to conclude that "there is little reason to wonder at the lack of deference which even the lowliest freshman seems to accord his party leaders. Respect, trust, and accommodation are readily demonstrated, but very little awe or excessive veneration is apparent."[10] Fifty years earlier, George Rothwell Brown came to the same conclusion and stated it with unusual bluntness: "The facts are that there has never been any leadership in the Senate."[11]

Leadership positions are also now very widely dispersed in the House, with almost 300 people who chair or are ranking minority members on one standing committee or subcommittee or another. That is a remarkable dispersion of leadership resources, but that leaves more than a quarter of the membership—typically the most junior—with no leadership position. Compare this to the Senate, where newly elected senators of the majority party present their certificates of election and are usually handed gavels. They may have spent their entire adult lives before coming to the Senate selling software or plywood, or piloting a Boeing 727, but would literally have to shun leadership to prevent its being thrust on them.

Perhaps the greatest contrast in how the leadership in the House and Senate are regarded by members can be found in the testimony of those people who served only briefly in the House and never gained much seniority and were then elected to the Senate. One senator who had this experience was Montana Democrat Max S. Baucus, who recalled, "I was a very junior member when I was in the House and the leadership was very remote to me. I've been here longer but there are also only one hundred of us and Bob Byrd, and Bob Dole, and Howard Baker are very approachable. I'm even friends with them. I never had that in the House."

While leadership in the House is vastly more member oriented and supportive of the rank-and-file than at any time in history, there is a discernible pyramid of hierarchy in the House that one does not find in the Senate. A Senate leader, indeed, can be likened to a lieutenant-general in an army composed only of major-generals or to the chair of an academic department in which all the faculty members are on lifetime tenure. So while House leaders rarely act in a high-handed and authoritarian manner with ordinary members, Senate leaders almost never do.

An analogy that might be used to describe the different relationships between leadership and members in the House and Senate is an ecclesiastical one: The House leader ministers to a flock; the Senate leader more nearly resembles the chaplain in a medieval court whose ministrations were highly personalized and phrased with the delicacy and diplomacy that acknowledges the power and vanity of his communicants.

An Epidemic of Staff: The Unelected
Leading the Overburdened

The size differences that give rise to Senate generalism and House specialization influence profoundly the role of staff members in both chambers. At the most basic level, it is important to note that senators' personal staffs are larger than the personal staffs of the House members. House members are entitled by House rules to hire eighteen full-time and four part-time employees. The average House member has an office staff of fifteen. The average Senate staff is thirty-one, but according to Senate rules senators are given staff allowances based on the population of their state. Accordingly, a senator from California or New York might have more than seventy assistants.[12]

In addition to personal staff, House chairmen and subcommittee chairmen and ranking minority members have professional staff to help them with the business of their committees,
and since 1975, even the most junior senator has had committee
staff assigned to him.

Spread so thinly across a range of committees whose subject
matters may differ widely, the senator's relationship to staff is
far different from that of the more focused House member.
Because their ability to develop specialized knowledge is limited
by the time that they can devote to any one committee responsibility, senators must rely on staff to fill in the gaps.

But senators can also tackle a wider range of national issues;
they gain broader exposure through their multiple committee
assignments and are generally less constrained than House
members on the topics on which they can speak. Liberal rules
of debate permit them to use the floor as a forum to raise new
issues that need not even be related to pending legislation. Staff
provides them with many of these issues.

Finally, the Senate has always been the "nursery of presidents." Sixteen senators have gone on to the presidency, and in
every recent campaign a senator has been a major contender for
one party or the other for the presidential nomination. The
1988 campaign produced as candidates Senator Bob Dole on
the Republican side and Senators Joseph Biden, Albert Gore,
Paul Simon, and former senator Gary Hart on the Democratic
side. The last incumbent House member to be elected directly
to the presidency was James A. Garfield in 1880, and U.S.
representatives are more unusual figures on the presidential
scene. Republican Jack Kemp and Democrat Richard Gephardt represented the House in the 1988 campaign but dropped
out by the end of March of that year.

While there are restrictions against using congressional staff
in presidential campaigns, it is a prohibition that is easily
evaded. With their smaller staffs, House members lack the
built-in advantage that senators have in mounting a national
campaign. Few House members, moreover, have the national

visibility enjoyed by senators and so they find it difficult to develop such an image given the limitation of staff resources.[13]

But even in the normal course of legislative business, the differences in the prominence of staff as between the House and Senate are obvious. Viewers of the televised floor action in both houses rarely get a shot of a senator without a staffer close at hand. Normally forbidden to take staff onto the floor with them, House members engage in solitary combat, unsupported by staff retinues.

QUALITATIVE DIFFERENCES IN HOUSE AND SENATE STAFF

One surprising result from interviews with the senators who served in the House was that most of them simply considered Senate staff to be of better quality than House staff. The possibility that such a perception was held came up in one of the first interviews, with Senator Robert Taft, Jr. (R-Ohio). Taft felt that personal staff in the House tended to be "amateurs" while the "real pros" worked on the personal staff of senators. He felt that the "pros" on the House side were committee staff rather than those working in the personal office of the House member.

Senator William Hathaway echoed Taft's verdict but went further in explaining why there might be this qualitative difference.

The senators rely on them more heavily than the House members do, and I suppose you have a better chance of attracting good people with a six-year term than you have with a two-year term.

But it's also more responsibility. It's well known that senators give more responsibility to their staff than House members do.

Although the high rates of reelection of House members actually provide more job security for House staff, every one of the fourteen senators who had previously served in the House asserted that greater responsibilities were enjoyed by Senate staff. The broader responsibilities come from the fact that, in Senator John Culver's words, "senators are spread too thin and

are too distracted. They have too many committee responsibilities. They can't handle these things by themselves and they end
up relying excessively on staff." Culver added, "You have some
key House staffers who are with powerful members or assigned
to powerful committees who have influence comparable to or
greater than Senate staff. Generally speaking, however, for the
rank-and-file House members, there's just no comparison—
either delegated or usurped—[with what] staff members are
able to obtain or exercise on behalf of a senator."

Texas Republican Phil Gramm cited the larger size of Senate staffs as a factor contributing to their superiority over House
staffs.

Senate staffs are bigger and this allows for more specialization. So if
someone is going to talk to someone on my staff about a defense
matter, I have a person who does nothing but defense work. The
person went to Annapolis. They were in the navy. They were with the
CIA for five years and they flat know their business. Anything that
relates to national security and defense, we know about.

In the House there was no possibility that I could afford having
a staff member just to deal with defense, even if I had been on the
Armed Services Committee.

THE CAPTIVE SENATOR?

Because the senator is stretched thin and must delegate a
great deal more to aides than is typically the case with House
members, there is a danger of overdelegation. Every senator
seemed to have his own horror story of a colleague who had
become, in effect, a captive of his staff. Even after the passage
of many years, Senator Richard Schweiker's indignation at
such a captive senator had not cooled.

I won't use the guy's name, but I was working with a senator. We were
co-sponsors on a bill. There were actually four of us, so we got
together to work out some of our differences.

Well, we went to this senator's office who called the meeting and
he didn't do any of the talking. His staff guy was trying to run four
of us senators on this issue. I was just furious. I was really mad. This

senator just sat back and let his staff run us, and we all went away resolving that we'd never work with that S.O.B. again. Imagine: He delegated to his staff the entire job of working this thing out and he sat there and had his staff be the prominent players with four of his colleagues. It was an insult.

I couldn't conceive of that happening in the House. A lot of times I've seen that happen in the Senate. I just couldn't see it happening in the House.

The suggestion that senators were more apt to become captives of their staff because of the need to delegate more broadly came through in interviews with a group of twenty lobbyists. While none of the lobbyists doubted that a House member might well allow himself to be dominated by staff, all said that the most extreme cases were more apt to be found in the Senate.

A partner in a small but prestigious Washington firm had his own horror story.

We had a case in this Congress in which we'd reached a point where we were having trouble with a particular senator. Our client's outside staff counsel had gone to school with this senator—college roommate types. So the client called me and asked if we minded having his outside counsel talk to the senator directly because things weren't where they should have been. I said, "Hell, no, I'll take all the help I can get in bringing this guy around."

So this senator says to his buddy of twenty-five years' standing, "I'm okay on this issue, but you've got a problem with my staff." A most revealing comment, right? He was saying, I agree with you but my staff doesn't, and therefore you have a problem.

A lobbyist for a major pharmaceutical firm discerned a type of staffer on the House side that he said was uncommon in the Senate: the "note taker." "They sit and listen to your pitch and ask questions and tell you that another lobbyist has been in arguing the other side and what do you say to that and when they're pressed for their boss's position, they back off. You just don't find that type very often in the Senate."

Senators, lobbyists, and staff members alike seem to agree that Senate staffs have longer "leashes"—more latitude, more freedom to negotiate on behalf of their bosses—and, not surprisingly, are more likely to end up "downtown" as high-priced lobbyists or officials in the executive branch. Indeed, a study by Robert Salisbury and Kenneth Shepsle found that there was a higher staff turnover in the "fast track" of the Senate than there was among House staff members. House staff, particularly those working on standing committees, are more likely to be Capitol Hill lifers.[14]

If tomorrow all congressional staff disappeared, the House would be far better able to conduct its business than the Senate. With identical coverage of public policy, legislative responsibility, and oversight but with four and a half times the manpower and vastly greater specialized knowledge in the membership, the House would carry on. Barring some drastic limitations on the way senators currently spend their time and energy, the smaller body would simply be unable to cope with its burdens.

But while Senate staff is more influential, in general, than House staff, and even considering cases of staff dominance on the Senate side, the ultimate source of authority is the senator. The fact that most office-to-office contact on the Senate side is at the staff level should not obscure the fact that on important issues there is consultation between the principals. On nonroutine matters, the ground rules are established by the senators. In the words of an administrative assistant to a freshman senator, "It's *mano a mano*"—a hand-to-hand struggle between the principals.

Size and the Management of Conflict

Forging a consensus in the small and individualistic Senate under a system of rules whereby each senator has what amounts to a qualified veto has caused some observers to pronounce the Senate unmanageable. Without a question, the Senate is a highly inefficient body. But it must be recalled that if efficiency had been highly prized by the framers of the Constitution they probably would have created a one-house Congress. Indeed, the framers feared hasty action and the tendency of a majority to ride roughshod over the rights of minorities. The Senate is a shrine to the rights of the political minority and its rules confer considerable power on it to thwart the will of the majority.

Armed with such imposing power, each senator becomes an enforcer of the rights of the interests he or she represents. Like ambassadors from sovereign kingdoms, senators face one another as legal equals. Coercive tactics are inappropriate for such encounters, so consensus building through face-to-face contacts is the preferred method for managing conflict.

This produces two results—one institutional and one with implications for the larger political system.

The institutional result of face-to-face contact in a small Senate and the group-to-group contact in a large House of Representatives is that any given senator is much more likely to know any other senator than a House member is to know any other colleague. This firsthand knowledge of a colleague's background and constituency tends to deemphasize partisan or ideological traits. Close encounters of a personal kind can also lead to terrible vendettas, but the compactness of the Senate chamber leaves combatants few places to hide. There is a strong incentive toward damage control in the relationships among senators. House members, like air crews dropping bombs on an enemy they cannot see, take a more cold-blooded view of partisan warfare. You can drop your bombs and then retire to the vastness of a huge membership. Avoidance of hostile colleagues in the House is as easy as surrounding yourself with a group that is friendly. The rules of engagement in the Senate are largely personal; in the House they are distinctively partisan.

The implications for national politics is that the Senate is able to manage conflict somewhat more readily than the House. The consensus arrived at in the Senate on a given issue is virtually assured of having been at least influenced by the minority because of each member's equal powers within that body. The Senate, as an institution, stands more solidly behind its work product, which is perhaps one reason that less specialized senators fare so well in conference committees. A House member can claim to have been left out of a decision by reason of having been in a minority whose views were swept aside; that is a more difficult assertion for a senator to make. The legislation that comes out of the Senate, then, can be said to reflect a broader range of opinion.

House members who represent fewer interests than senators can articulate these issues more efficiently and often do so more forcefully and passionately. This contributes to the adversary style of the House. Spared the necessity to keep interpersonal relations in good repair to the extent that senators must, House members can express interests with passion and even ferocity. But the passion with which an interest is advocated has little to do with whether that interest is reflected in the legislation that comes out of the chamber.

The Senate is a more unitary body than the House not because political conflict is absent but because the minority side is more likely to have had an impact on its legislation than the minority side within the House. The Senate tends to be a place of concurrent majorities where all major segments of opinion need to concur but not necessarily be represented in the proportions in which they are found in the general public.

The House's role is to allow interests to be represented and articulated. It makes no representations that they will be influential or even heeded. It is a better reflection of the diversity of the country than is the Senate. The House is able to pick up, with almost seismographic sensitivity, what it is that is eating at Americans. Using a different metaphor, Senator Donald Riegle said, "If on any given day, you wanted to take the temperature of the country, all you'd need to do would be to take the temperature of the House of Representatives and you'd get a pretty good reading of what the country is thinking."

In a mass society in which citizens fear that government is slipping out of their grasp, the House remains accessible to citizens—it deals with their problems and opinions. It is, however, less good in its original role of being the place where citizens could register their objections to national policies through periodic elections. The Senate, we shall see, is not only the more unitary body of the two; it is also the more responsive.

NOTES

1. John R. Cranford, "Party Unity Scores Slip in 1988, But Overall Pattern Is Upward," *Congressional Quarterly Weekly Report,* Vol. 46, No. 47, p. 3334.
2. See Gregory A. Caldeira and Samuel C. Patterson, "Political Friendship in the Legislature," a *Polimetrics* reprint (Columbus: Laboratory for Political and Social Research, n.d.), p. 963.
3. David E. Rosenbaum, "Do's and Don't of Party Cooperation," *New York Times,* Tuesday, October 27, 1987.
4. Ibid.
5. Ibid.
6. Jeffrey H. Birnbaum, "How Three Legislators Wheeled and Dealed to Help Draft Tax Bill," *Wall Street Journal,* Tuesday, November 26, 1985.
7. Barbara Sinclair, *Majority Leadership in the U.S. House* (Baltimore, Md.: Johns Hopkins Press, 1983).
8. Woodrow Wilson, *Congressional Government* (Boston: Houghton-Mifflin, 1885), p. 213.
9. Neil MacNeil, *Forge of Democracy* (New York: David McKay, 1963), p. 376.
10. Robert L. Peabody, *Leadership in Congress* (Boston: Little, Brown, 1976), pp. 346–347.
11. George Rothwell Brown, *The Leadership in Congress* (Indianapolis, Ind.: Bobbs-Merrill, 1922), p. 254.
12. Roger H. Davidson and Walter J. Oleszek, *Congress and Its Members,* 2d ed. (Washington, D.C.: CQ Press, 1985), p. 245.
13. Malcolm E. Jewell and Samuel C. Patterson, *The Legislative Process in the United States,* 4th ed. (New York: Random House, 1986), p. 157.
14. Robert H. Salisbury and Kenneth A. Shepsle, "Congressional Staff Turnover and the Ties-That-Bind," *American Political Science Review,* 75 (June 1981), pp. 393–394, and Michael J. Malbin, *Unelected Representatives* (New York: Basic, 1980), pp. 86–87.

4

The Electoral Environments

THERE IS A RELATIONSHIP between House members and the roughly 550,000 people who make up their constituencies that the members speak of using words that we do not ordinarily associate with politics. They speak of "empathy" and "trust" in the relations with their constituents, and of "identifying" with them.[1] It is a language of intimacy and it flows naturally from the bond between a representative and a manageable political unit—the congressional district.

Some congressional districts are more complex than others. House members, moreover, do not experience the same degree of intimacy with their staunchest and most loyal supporters as they do with people who just happen to live in the district, but overall the relationships between House members and their districts and those between senators and their states are strikingly different. The most basic difference comes from the fact that House members can figuratively get their hands around a district. The senators interviewed spoke of an almost tactile sensation when describing techniques they used with their former House constituencies. Such feelings of intimacy are rare when a complete state is the constituency. Of the fourteen senators who formerly served in the House and were interviewed for this book, only the four who came from states with only two House seats reported little or no decline in these feelings of intimacy after reaching the Senate. Senators James Abourezk and George McGovern of South Dakota, Max Baucus of Montana, and William Hathaway of Maine represented roughly half of the state and their transfer to the Senate was a change only in degree rather than an entirely novel experience.

The feeling of monumental change was, naturally enough, greatest in senators who had formerly represented districts in very populous states. Hugh Scott and Richard Schweiker of Pennsylvania and Phil Gramm of Texas emphasized the dramatic quality of the transition. But the transition was also significant and noteworthy in senators from geographically small states with relatively large numbers of districts. One of these is Christopher Dodd—for him, the difference in intimacy between representing one of his state's six congressional districts and representing the entire state of Connecticut was summed up in how he spent his Saturday nights.

You're back in your district and on a Saturday night there might be, let's say, three events. And you'll go to two of them and you'll stay almost a couple of hours at each one. You'd be there for the cocktail hour, the dinner, the speeches, and even hanging around afterwards to say goodnight to the people.

In the Senate you might do three events on a Saturday night, but at one place you'll go to the cocktail hour and give a speech. And the next place you'll go to the dinner and you'll stand and wave from the podium because you've got to get to the next one. It's so detached. It's a terribly difficult transition to make if you've gotten very tactile and hands-on with your constituency. When you get to the Senate you've got to step back.

John Culver, who represented Iowa, spoke of the "intimacy and personal rapport" a House member establishes with his or her district, which is "extremely hard to duplicate on a statewide basis." He said, "You really have genuine personal contacts of familiarity. These people are your neighbors. You really get to know them and they know you."

Senator Donald Riegle, who represents Michigan, said, "Having a constituency of roughly half a million people is a good size constituency in the sense that you could get your hands around a constituency that size and have a level of contact and intimacy that I value and miss."

The loss of intimacy expressed by so many of the House-members-turned-senators bears closer examination. Are they lamenting, literally, the diminished ability to relate to a larger, more amorphous, and more heterogeneous constituency as individuals? Without question, there is a reluctance on the part of large-state senators to exchange the handshaking of one-on-one campaigning characteristic of House elections for the "wholesale" politicking on statewide television. One gets a sense from a study based on observations and interviews of House members that personal contact and handshaking constituted for them a superior form of campaigning. Even one who recognized the need to use television in a statewide campaign expressed fear that he might be cast as a "celluloid candidate" by reason of his extensive use of the medium and insisted on at least some personal campaigning.[2]

Senators can, then, continue to make dawn visits to factory gates and shake hands personally with the voters even if only for the benefit of the cameras. Where conditions permit, most typically in races in small or low-population states, some senators attempt to duplicate in their campaigns the personal techniques they used as House members. In the most populous states you simply cannot shake enough hands to make much difference in an election.

In addition to the sense of intimacy experienced by House members toward their constituencies, the average congressional district is simply more knowable than the average state and these differences in complexity figure importantly in the electoral environments of House members and senators.

Differences in State and District Complexity: The Political Implications

The typical House district, even a complex one, is, of course, of more limited scope than an entire state. It is a smaller and less prominent stage on which to perform. And district lines are subject to adjustment every ten years to accommodate census changes, so there is an evanescent quality to the congressional district—something like a tent that can be folded up and moved. A state is permanent. It may gain or lose population, become prosperous or wither economically, but its borders are sacrosanct.

Each state is like a circus big top—lots of acts going on at the same time, a jumble of activity, cacophonous, and busy. A host of economic interests vie for the favor of government and legions of associations, ethnic groups, and political actors cavort on the sawdust.

Some congressional districts approximate this theatrical model, but most are places where interests run in a narrower track, where a single racial or ethnic group may be dominant, where a handful of large industries account for most of the payrolls. They are the sideshows, the specialty acts. They are off the midway and not likely to be recognized by the casual observer. The crossing of any state line is usually heralded by a sign welcoming you, but one would search in vain for a sign that says "Welcome to the 4th Congressional District."

In most instances the very scope of the state in terms of geographical size, diversity, size of population, and multiplicity of interests creates greater political complexity than that which typically confronts a member of the House. The implications of this greater complexity differ from state to state but generally they present senators with choices—often of a politically treacherous nature—that House members do not have to confront.

Norris Cotton, a Republican who represented New Hampshire in the House and Senate, wrote in his memoirs shortly after his 1975 retirement that the greater complexity of states is a product of greater political and economic diversity. To illustrate, he observed, "Urban [congressional] districts are usually overwhelmingly Democratic; they are liberal, and largely dominated by organized labor. Rural districts tend to be Republican; they are conservative and principally engaged in small business and agriculture. There are, of course, a certain number of borderline districts that swing back and forth. These are mostly suburban domains . . . [but] a majority of members of the House of Representatives come from districts that are solidly one way or the other."[3]

The implication of this for Cotton was that the "congressman is chosen because his political philosophy is in tune with that of the overwhelmingly majority of his constituents and this makes his task comparatively simple. He votes his own convictions, which happily coincide with the convictions of those he represents."[4]

States are less simple both in political and partisan terms. There are congressional districts in which one party or the other is simply not able to compete and so these districts have been in the hands of representatives of one party for as long as anyone can remember. Only about one-quarter of all House seats are truly competitive. In very few states is one party so uncompetitive in Senate contests that election of the other party's candidate is deemed a foregone conclusion. Perhaps Massachusetts for the Democrats and Idaho or Utah for the Republicans are such bastions, but states like these are few in number. The primary reason for this is that the boundaries of House districts are subject to manipulation for political purposes and state boundaries are not. Particularly if a state has gained or lost House seats as the result of changes in population, the state legislature must redraw district boundaries. This reconstruction of a state's congressional district map is usually calculated to protect incumbent House members. Both the Democratic and Republican House members make sure to keep their relations with state legislators in good repair.[5]

Given the intensely political nature of redistricting and the results of demographic changes, many districts are not nearly so neat as Senator Cotton describes. With the Supreme Court's requirement that congressional districts within a state vary minimally in population, lines are sometimes drawn in such a way as to throw together into a district communities that have little in common. But even if congressional districts are not so homogeneous as they may have been before the Court insisted on districts of precisely the same populations, few can boast the diversity found in a state.

THE SENATORIAL TERRAIN:
AN ELEMENT OF RISK

In the minds of some senators additional political risks come with greater diversity and complexity. There is even a kind of envy of the relatively uncomplicated political environment in which House members operate. Senator Paul Sarbanes, a Maryland Democrat who represented an urban district in Baltimore when he was in the House, seemed to reflect this view when he said of House members: "If your views are basically in line with those of your district you've got a lot of freedom. And even if they're not, you can usually make up for it through your constituency casework and developing a personal rapport with your district. That is much more difficult to do if you are a senator."

What Sarbanes is suggesting is that House members need only concern themselves with the limited range of issues that are of importance to their district. The many issues that a senator must confront in a considerably more complicated state make it virtually impossible to be "right" on all the issues.

The specifics of the greater complexity that awaits House members when they move to the Senate and confront statewide problems were supplied by Pennsylvania Republicans Hugh Scott and Richard Schweiker. Scott had represented an urban Philadelphia district and Schweiker a prosperous suburban Philadelphia constituency. For both, representing the more complex state meant a great adjustment. Scott, as a congressman, had pretty much restricted himself to "the social problems that come with an urban district: health, welfare, the environment, mass transit, and highways. With the state you still have those but you pick up agriculture, mining, and the impact of large, well-organized, powerful unions." Schweiker's district "did have a steel mill, but it was basically, even predominantly, a white-collar suburban district."

The complexity, by itself, required adaptation on the part of both former House members, but the new diversity carried with it an ominous and intimidating quality as well. In Scott's words, "I also picked up a much wider and more skillful collection of adversaries." The transition from the relatively simple congressional district to the generally more complex state involves, then, not only a greater and more bewildering array of interests but a broader range of potential antagonists and opponents. For these two Republicans from affluent districts in the Philadelphia area, organized labor had not been an important factor. Pennsylvania's blue-collar unions, which were a major political force statewide, traditionally supported Democrats and while neither Scott nor Schweiker was hostile to labor, the unions would have felt more comfortable with Democrats.

Stephen K. Bailey's classic study of the passage of the union-endorsed Employment Act of 1946 pointed to the differential impact of union influence in the two houses of Congress. He wrote, "As the political power of organized labor has grown . . . and as population movements into the cities have increased, it has become increasingly difficult for Senators . . . to ignore the interests and demands of the urban worker. A Representative from the 17th District in Illinois, for example, may find it possible to disregard the voice of the urban worker; a Senator representing the entire state, would do so only at considerable peril to his political future."[6]

All senators interviewed agreed that only a few issues arising out of the more complex senatorial constituency forced them to make choices they did not have to make in their House districts. Nonetheless, difficult political decisions that force senators to have to choose between the interests of one group of constituents and those of another are part of the job for every senator whose state is at all complex.

Senator George A. Smathers, a Democrat who represented Florida in the Senate from 1951 until 1969 after serving two years in the House, contrasted the simplicity and parochialism of the interests of his south Florida district with the complexities of the entire state of Florida.

With congressmen it's all local. Everything is more local—the local post office, the local industry, the local river, the local airport, the local Miami harbor. Why, if I could get the money to deepen the Miami harbor from fourteen to twenty-one feet, that alone would come damn near to getting me reelected.

But at the state level, Miami not only wanted it, but Jacksonville wanted it, Cape Canaveral wanted it, and Pensacola wanted it. And you know that all of them can't get it. You've got bigger, broader problems covering a wider spectrum of people.

Smathers cited two problems in particular that confronted him as a senator that had not troubled him as a member of the House and which arose from the size and diversity of his new constituency. The first was that, in the 1950s, divisions among many Floridians on civil rights were acute. Smathers recalled:

My Miami district was very liberal. It was a town with a lot of foreign-born and minority groups. There was a large Jewish community and a lot of sophisticated people from New York had moved down. Their attitude on civil rights would be classified as liberal.

But you go to Crestview, Florida, which is the county seat of Okaloosa County, which is out in the panhandle, they're old cracker folks. Or in Gadsden County that abuts Georgia—country Georgia. The civil rights situation there is a different thing completely.

In the bitterly fought Florida Senate primary in 1950, not only did Smathers modify his previous stand on civil rights, he characterized incumbent Claude Pepper as being excessively friendly to blacks. Once in the Senate, in Smathers' words, "There was an adjustment in my record. I voted against the so-called civil rights bills such as the one in 1957. Now looking at it from heaven down, you'd know I was wrong. Looking at it as a practical political situation, I could not have gotten elected. I couldn't have gotten the votes in north and central Florida if I'd voted for those civil rights bills."

In the 1940s, J. William Fulbright represented a House district in northwestern Arkansas with few blacks and consequently little racial antagonism. He felt confident championing the cause of a black civil servant who had a dispute with the Treasury Department, but that gesture in those days of racial animosity caused Fulbright serious, though not insurmountable, problems when he ran for the Senate statewide because the rest of the state more nearly reflected the deep racial divisions of the South than did his district.

George Smathers recalled that on a bill less momentous than the civil rights bill, a proposal to build a barge canal across the state of Florida, he was thrust into a conflict of a kind unknown when he was in the House. While a House member from south Florida, he could stand with his Dade County constituents who were adamantly opposed to the project. Northern Floridians just as fervently approved of the canal. As Smathers recalls, "One of my first votes on coming to the Senate [was] in favor of the canal. It caused me many, many political problems. I just felt that I was serving the larger constituency and the better interest of the state."

Smathers' comments reflect an attitude that typified all but one senator—that the increase in scope and complexity of the state over the House district did pose increased challenges and choices, but that such problems came with the territory and had to be met head-on if one were to be a successful senator. As Senator Phil Gramm put it with characteristic bluntness: "If you can't make a political decision, you're not going to last long in the Senate."

THE LOSS OF CONTROL: A SENATORIAL LAMENT

There is an unmistakable theme in the testimony of the senators who were interviewed that the House district was responsive to them and under their control to the extent that a state was not. It is as if by the laying on of hands House members can take the pulse of the district and apply the proper political therapy. They lose this when they exchange a district for a statewide constituency and many of them miss it.

A few of the senators, unprompted, went beyond their lamentations of the loss of intimacy to broach what may be the hidden issue: The state is less controllable an entity from a political standpoint. After decrying the loss of intimacy with constituents that attended his move to the Senate, one interviewee said, "What I'm getting at is that there is more uncertainty. The senate seat is by definition more precarious politically than the average House seat." Senator Paul Sarbanes found that the greater attention lavished on senators by the media and the relative obscurity of the activities of House members was a situation that favored the political fortunes of the House member. He put it this way:

In the Senate, you're dependent on that intermediary to a much greater degree—the press, television are on you a lot. You need the TV coverage to reach statewide but it interferes with the message you put out to the voters.

South Dakota's James Abourezk put the district-state difference simply and directly. "House members have a good sense of what their district is. Senators have a harder time getting a handle on a state and it makes them more destructible than House members."

Presentation of self to the voters is generally much more under the control of the House member than of the senator. As Morris P. Fiorina observed in the late 1970s, "Congressmen are going home more, pressing the flesh, getting around. They are building a personal base of support, one dependent on personal contacts and favors."[7]

The very compactness and relative simplicity of most congressional districts, the relatively scant attention paid by the media to members in multidistrict states (and to their challengers as well), the unlikelihood that the member will be presented with serious political conflicts, and the ability to meet the voters

directly present a political landscape of greater serenity to the
House member. Large and complex states can foster more challengers, harbor more regional or interest group conflicts, and
bathe senators in media attention that they may be able to
control only imperfectly.

House-Senate Elections:
The Blessings of Obscurity

The observations of the former House members who won
Senate seats that the district is a more controllable and manipu-
lable political environment than the state receive confirmation
on the different rates of success that members and senators
enjoy in winning reelection. In only two elections since World
War II has the percentage of senators gaining reelection been
higher than that of House members seeking another term. It
happened most recently in 1982, a recession year in which
Democrats gained twenty-six House seats and many ousted
members had been elected on Ronald Reagan's coattails in
1980. In other big-turnover years, such as 1964 and 1974, when
more than fifty House seats changed hands, Senate reelection
percentages exceeded those of the House, but it is normal for
the reelection rate of House members to be much higher than
for senators. In 1976, 1978, and 1980 House reelection percentages were more than 30 points better than Senate success rates.
And for the forty years between 1946 and 1986, the average
reelection percentage for Senate incumbents was a respectable
74.9 percent. For House members, however, the figure was
close to 91 percent.[8]

The most basic reason for the relatively greater degree of
success for House incumbents over Senate incumbents is that
senators are just larger, more visible, and more inviting targets.
The size differential between the two chambers accounts for
much of the quandary of the sitting senator becoming the sitting duck. For ideological groups to be able to claim that their

contributions led to the defeat of 9 members of a body of 100 is a far more impressive boast than that they unseated 9 members in a body of 435. One is unlikely to see a hunter returning home with the fenders of his car festooned with squirrel carcasses but he will proudly display a single moose or deer.

The apparent success in 1980 of an organization called the National Conservative Political Action Committee (NCPAC) illustrates the political payoff that comes from targeting incumbent senators. Beginning more than a year before the 1980 election, NCPAC ultimately put together a war chest of $1.2 million to defeat senators that the group characterizes as "the most distasteful."[9] This group included such familiar Democrats as Frank Church of Idaho, John Culver of Iowa, and Birch Bayh of Indiana as well as the 1972 Democratic presidential candidate George McGovern, who had continued his Senate career after suffering defeat at the hands of President Richard M. Nixon.

While the Republicans were stunningly successful in gaining thirty-three House seats in 1980—giving the House the largest number of Republicans since 1956—it was the ousting of the nine Democratic senators that NCPAC and other conservative groups regarded as their signal of triumph. Eighty percent of the money spent by the so-called "independent-expenditure" groups in 1980 went for negative campaigns directed against Senate Democrats. The House elections in 1980 showed the reverse pattern of expenditures by these groups, with most money being spent on behalf of incumbents, but in 1982 House Democrats were targeted by conservative groups in an effort that proved counterproductive in an election that saw Democrats gain twenty-six seats. The Democrats had been expected to win even more seats in that recession year, but adopted a defensive strategy designed to protect incumbents rather than support challengers—a clear reaction to the reverses suffered by House Democrats in 1980.[10]

Groups opposed to abortion—only one of the constellation of issues that animated NCPAC—developed a strategy for 1980

that would enable them to be depicted as "giant-killers" if they
directed their efforts to the defeat of well-known liberal Democratic senators. These groups got "more bang for the buck" in
their campaigns against incumbent senators than they would
have against incumbent House members. Put another way, "It
would take a brave group to announce its intention to defeat
one-sixth of the *House* members up for reelection; during the
past decade, at least 90 percent of all House incumbents who
ran for reelection won their contests. Groups aiming at senators
would have a clearer shot; only 60 percent of senators seeking
reelection in 1978 were successful."[11]

While some people minimize the effect of NCPAC on the
defeat of the liberal senators in 1980, few doubt that the strategy
of John T. "Terry" Dolan, chairman of the NCPAC, was to
focus on the Senate races because of the visibility of the targets.
Peter Fenn, a Washington political consultant, worked in 1980
for Frank Church, the Idaho Democrat who was one of those
"most distasteful" senators. Fenn asserts that lesser known
House members as targets would have made NCPAC's job of
raising money from conservative givers much more difficult.

Dolan's whole idea was that the Senate was the place you found those
crazy, fuzzy-headed liberals and his pitch was that you have to get rid
of these wackos. The people that Dolan appealed to knew and hated
the Frank Churches, and Birch Bayhs, and George McGoverns. They
wouldn't have known Les Au Coin [a liberal Democratic House
member] from Adam. The only way Dolan could raise money was
with those [senators] as targets. That's how Dolan got on the CBS
Evening News and in *Newsweek* because he was dealing with the
Senate and those guys who were well-enough known and his direct
mail was going like gangbusters based on that strategy.

While there is unanimous agreement that the "incumbent
advantage" redounds much more to the benefit of House members than to senators, there are a number of plausible explanation about why this difference is so marked. The incumbent
advantage is far more formidable, as we have seen, in House
elections since the deck can be stacked by a state legislature in

the way it draws congressional district lines to favor incumbents. States are not subject to that kind of manipulation for political purposes. And while the distribution of a state's electorate cannot be manipulated against incumbent senators, neither can it be rigged in their favor.

Partisanship has also become an increasingly uncertain force in what lever the voter pulls in a voting booth during a congressional election. A CBS/New York Times poll of 1,062 registered adult voters just before the 1986 congressional elections explored their motivations and why they preferred one House candidate over another. More than 40 percent of those questioned said that the character and experience of the candidate counted most in their choice. Roughly a quarter said it was state or local issues, but only 9 percent pointed to a House candidate's party label as making the biggest difference in how they cast their vote.[12] Such surveys reinforce a point made by Thomas Mann and Raymond Wolfinger: "Party plays an important role for some voters in determining whether a candidate is attractive . . . but it is secondary to the images of the candidates themselves."[13]

Mann and Wolfinger make a further point that in elections in which voters emphasize character and experience, or at least the image of it, it is incumbents that benefit. Incumbents are seen as more visible and more attractive to voters than challengers. Indeed, 90 percent of all voters reported some contact with a House incumbent but only 44 percent reported contact with a House challenger.[14]

One reason for the positive image enjoyed by House incumbents that Mann and Wolfinger cite is the advantage of office. They enjoy, for example, the use of "franking privileges," the ability to send out printed materials free of postage. They are also in a position to intervene on behalf of constituents needing assistance in dealing with government. The newsletters, releases, ceremonial appearances, and occasions for symbolic but politically powerful gestures do weigh heavily in favor of the House incumbent.[15]

At least as compelling an ingredient for House incumbents'

success according to Mann and Wolfinger is that House members rarely receive serious challenges. Senators, however, seem to be less able than House members to convert their incumbency into invulnerability. "Most Senate challengers," they say, "are big spenders and run competitive races, while the vast majority of House challengers have small budgets and even smaller chances of winning."[16]

Mann and Wolfinger offer two explanations for the inadequacy of challenges to House incumbents and the more competitive Senate challenges. The first is that there are so many districts with lopsided partisan majorities that upsets by minority party challengers are unlikely. They also point to the readiness and ability of well-funded Senate challengers to use the media—notably television—to make themselves known to voters. Many House districts—notably those in large urban areas—do not lend themselves to the use of television. Advertising rates in such metropolitan areas are very high and since the districts themselves are small, a candidate would end up spending a great deal of money reaching voters who are unable to vote for him. Media coverage of House members and their challengers—as distinct from paid advertising—is also less extensive than that accorded to senators and their challengers. A New York television station would reach more than forty congressional districts in the New York/New Jersey/Connecticut metropolitan area. Adequate coverage of the activities of forty House members is impossible; adequate coverage of the activities of only six senators in those three states is relatively easy.

It is, perhaps, the "free media" difference between House and Senate challenges that contributes more to the differential rates of reelection success than paid campaign advertising. The differences in the attention paid to House members and senators in Washington by the national press will be covered in a later chapter, but it is the choice by the local media of whom they prefer to cover and whose activities and what issues they tend to emphasize that affects outcomes.

It is not just the greater number of members of the House

that makes coverage of their campaign less engrossing to the local media, but rather the nature of their activities. Over the past twenty-five years members of the House have not only emphasized constituent problem-solving and intervening on behalf of voters with the federal bureaucracy but actually stimulated the demands of citizens for these services, which range from nominating district youngsters to service academies to helping the elderly iron out problems with their T-bills with the Treasury Department's Bureau of Public Debt. Morris Fiorina uses the term ombudsmanship* to describe this effort by House members to be champions of their constituents.[17]

This casework, by its very nature, is uncontroversial. There are no right or wrong sides to using your power to nominate a high school senior to Annapolis. There is no political or moral downside to introducing a special immigration bill to reunite a family or to seeing that an old soldier gets the medical care he needs from a Veterans Administration hospital. Does this mean that by emphasizing service to constituents House members are being irresponsible or untrue to their duties as legislators, who must, by definition, also involve themselves in a lawmaking process that can involve supporting or casting votes on bills that are indeed controversial? While such votes constitute a minority of all votes that a member casts and are not an everyday occurrence, taking a controversial stand can alienate constituents; casework on behalf of constituents, however—unless it is bungled—involves no such risk.

While casework helps to establish a personal bond between members and voters, it is not an inherently interesting process. Except under special circumstances, journalists in the district would not cover the retrieval of a lost Social Security check or the mediation of a businessman's claim with the Small Business Administration. The very unspectacular nature of House members' activities enables them to reap a political dividend. "They

---

*The term *ombudsman* is a Swedish word that means, literally, "representative" but has come to mean a citizen advocate who intervenes on behalf of individuals who experience problems with government bureaucracies.

are able to focus constituents' attention on activities and personal attributes that will enhance their popularity. In other words, they successfully 'control' the information—limited, district-oriented and non-partisan in nature—that voters use to judge them."[18]

The administrative assistant to a New Jersey House member told me that the only time that casework activity drew extensive press coverage was during the Vietnam War when the congressman arranged for a helicopter to fly a shipment of Passover matzoh to a group of Jewish sailors on a U.S. Navy warship in the South China Sea. Wanting the traditional holiday food, the sailors asked their families to enlist the help of the congressman. The congressman's efforts brought wide and favorable publicity.

Voters also learn directly about the House members from the services they receive from them, and the message they receive is about caring, responsive officials who are not merely willing but eager to do battle on behalf of their constituents. So while only 46 percent of the nation's eligible voters in a 1982 Gallup poll were able to identify their House member by name, by a margin of nearly 4 to 1 those surveyed said their representative was doing a good job. Indeed, in all demographic groups in the survey a majority of people approved of the job their House member was doing.[19]

The local press, radio, and television, by their very neglect of the public stands and legislative activities of House members, serve, in effect, the political needs of those House members. They allow the members to tell their own stories to the voters in understandably self-serving ways. In contrast, it is the very newsworthiness of the senators that causes attention and scrutiny to fall upon them. This, as we have seen, contributed to the mortality rate among Senate Democrats in 1980. The attention, then, is very much a mixed blessing because it is not subject to the senator's control. Too many media are interested in senatorial activities, and although senators try to shape and direct the press to what they consider their most desirable activities, so much of what is said about them is beyond their manipulation.

Senators may issue press releases, but only the most uncritical journalists will be content to write a story based on a press handout. Senator Paul Sarbanes likened the media to "the eyes and ears of the public." Television, in particular, he said,

is like a conveyor belt between you and the constituents. But it's a conveyor belt that interposes itself in terms of what it asks and how it reports and you don't have that much control over it.

Senator Phil Gramm pointed out that in his own state of Texas, with its twenty-seven House seats, a member is unlikely to get coverage in media outside his own district, but "when you're representing the whole state every newspaper in the state is covering you as a local issue."

Senators appear, then, to be more associated in the public mind with major national issues than are House members. These matters are of more interest to the press, and word of senators' stands on issues filters back to the whole state. If senators take stands on divisive issues that are covered by the media back home, there can be a political price. As South Dakota Democrat James Abourezk put it:

Senate members, because their statements are picked up much more by the press than those of House members, are much more prone to controversy. In politics, the more controversy there is, the more enemies you make. The more enemies you make, the greater the chance of losing the election.

As already mentioned, the ways voters get to know senators and their challengers and House members and their opponents are quite distinct. Voter contact with House candidates is highly personal. Voters encounter the House candidates at coffees and small gatherings that promote eye contact and conversation. The encounters are reciprocal; communication flows in both directions. Senate candidates shake hands and attend town meetings but in large states they simply cannot do enough of this personal campaigning to have much impact. The communication by Senate candidates to voters is overwhelmingly through television. It is unilateral, impersonal, and establishes no firm bond. Yet senators are compelled to use it, and one study indicated that television advertising was almost twice as important to Senate incumbents as a way to contact voters as it was to House incumbents. And if senators use television to tell their story to the voters, the voters form their opinions of their senators from what they see of them on television.[20]

But television for senators is the classic two-edged sword. It provides for those seeking to unseat an incumbent a formidable siege weapon. Ironically, the TV ads of the challengers in Senate elections seem to be the single most influential way to shape voters' evaluations. They appear to be more decisive than ads run by the incumbents.[21]

House challengers are less apt to have the money to run TV ads, but when they do the ads appear not to have the impact that is achieved by those of Senate challengers. In fact, very little that House challengers can do in the way of advertising seems to be able to generate positive feelings about them in the minds of voters. Indeed, if there is a disadvantaged class of politicians in America it is House challengers. Even when they use a technique employed to good advantage by House incumbents, it seems to do little for them—mailings to voters work effectively to get voters to think well of House incumbents, but they appear to have little payoff for challengers.[22]

Below even the level of evaluation is the primitive level of awareness of candidates and here again the very abundance of information on Senate campaigns—largely from the electronic media—throws both challenger and incumbent into high resolution and clarity in the public mind. Such a deluge of information devalues face-to-face contact between senatorial candidate and voter. This is particularly the case in large and populous states such as California where a political rally in the 1986 campaign between incumbent senator Alan Cranston and Republican challenger Ed Zschau was described as "three people around a television set." Gerald Warren, editor of the *San Diego Union,* observed that neither Cranston nor Zschau would be found "at a shopping center or at a plant gate pressing the flesh."[23]

In contrast to a Senate campaign in the most populous and third-largest state in area is a House campaign in what is the geographically smallest congressional district, New York's 15th (known as the "Silk Stocking" district because of the affluence of many of its inhabitants), which extends down the East Side of Manhattan from 96th Street to the Bowery in lower Manhattan, a scant seven square miles. While there is now considerable contrast in wealth in the district between the glittering Upper East Side and the impoverished Lower East Side, it is strictly an urban district—no farms, no suburbs, and no defense plants. The median price for owning your living quarters in the district, however, is $185,000, the highest price for housing of any congressional district in the country due to its concentration of luxury condominiums, townhouses, and co-op apartments.[24]

In 1986, Democratic challenger George Hirsch shook an estimated 200,000 hands in his campaign in the 15th to unseat incumbent Republican Bill Green. Hirsch, who claimed to be running "a total retail campaign," had appeared so many times at the same subway station that one woman reportedly told him that "if he shook her hand once more they'd have to get engaged."[25] Green won the election because his stands on issues mirror those of his liberal constituents despite the fact that he is a Republican.

The Senate campaign, then, is fought on an electronic battlefield with the paid political spot being the weapon of choice for incumbent and challenger alike. House campaigns—except under unusual circumstances—tend to be more like hand-to-hand combat in which the combatant in office fights with both hands free and the challenger is hog-tied. The Senate battle, moreover, is a more equal and uncertain one where incumbents seem unable to come up with a tactical edge equivalent to that enjoyed by their House counterparts. The lack of media attention to House incumbents frees them to construct for themselves a positive political image among those voters who do know them. The same lack of media attention casts a shadow of obscurity on those who challenge members. Senate incum-

bents, to their political disadvantage, find that the very lime-
light in which they bask also illuminates those who seek to
dislodge them.

ISSUES AND POLICY IN HOUSE AND
SENATE ELECTIONS

We have seen that the greater complexity of the statewide
political environment presents senators with much more uncertainty and considerably less control over events than House
incumbents encounter with their simpler and more circumscribed congressional districts. At least part of this uncertainty
for senators seems to be associated with the higher public pro-
file they achieve, relative to House members. Recognizing that
senators are more visible and that their visibility may, paradoxically, give stature to their challengers does not in itself provide
a very complete picture of the differences in senator-representa-
tive vulnerability.

Does the visibility of the office of senator, or the senatorial
election by itself, produce vulnerability or is there a difference
in the very subject matter over which House and Senate elections are fought that influences the different rates of electoral
success for incumbents?

The 1978 Michigan Election Study suggests that there may
be profound differences between House and Senate elections in
terms of the importance of policies—economic policies in particular.

James H. Kuklinski and Darrell M. West, using data from
the Michigan study, concluded that neither those voters who
saw their personal financial situations as having improved nor
those who saw their income status as having deteriorated indicated that these economic changes had much to do with their
choice of one Senate or House candidate over another. When
the question, however, became what the future held for the
economic well-being of voters, Kuklinski and West concluded
that voters did indeed let their concerns for the future influence
their choices in Senate elections. When asked about their expec-

tations for the upcoming year and how this would affect their choice of a Democratic or Republican Senate candidate, the pessimists, midway in the administration of Democratic president Jimmy Carter, indicated that they would support the Republican senate candidates. Those who were more upbeat about their economic future showed stronger support for Democratic Senate candidates. Significantly, however, predictions about the immediate economic future seemed to have little influence on whether a voter would opt for a Democrat or Republican in a House contest.[26]

Kuklinski and West, taking note of the fact that "House members have more successfully than their Senate counterparts isolated themselves from in-party economic performance, principally by establishing their roles as ombudsmen and providers of individualized services," conclude that a party-blind vote for a House member is probably a rational act from the voter's point of view inasmuch as "the individual voter . . . has benefitted from personalized [House member] services in the past—and expects to benefit in the future."[27] While they stop short of saying that senators alone are held to account for the policies of the president whose party affiliation they share, Kuklinski and West do seem to suggest that if senators chose to imitate House members in the provision of services and ombudsmenship, it would reduce their vulnerability to defeat. Many senators, of late, appear to be heeding this precept by assigning larger numbers of staff members to constituent problems and locating them in offices in the state. This would also, of course, reduce greatly the vulnerability of legislators on policy matters and make them answerable only for the effective delivery of government services.[28] It raises questions of how well citizens can register their indignation with failing presidential policies in midterm elections if both the House members *and* the senators from the president's party become insulated from voter reprisal. And what of the ability of a newly elected president to claim a policy mandate when he fails to pull in House members and senators of his own party? George Bush experienced this coattail problem in 1988 when only two Democratic House incumbents and one Democratic senator were defeated.

Responsiveness and the Two Democracies

The apparent fact that senators may be held to a more rigorous standard of policy accountability than House members has important implications in terms of the two expressions of democracy. Congressional elections are the only opportunity for a referendum on presidential performance other than the presidential elections themselves. In midterm elections when the president does not head the ticket, congressional elections have been the device that voters could use to register approval or disapproval of presidential performance. But House elections seem to be declining as a barometer of popular feelings about national policy. With House incumbents enjoying an average reelection rate of 95 percent in the five most recent elections, it is hard to argue that such contests are much of a referendum. Senators, however, with their lower reelection rate of 75 percent, seem to be the national officeholders from whom responsiveness is being demanded.

House members can, if they wish, align themselves quite comfortably with the simpler array of interests in their districts and take refuge behind House procedures that minimize embarrassing or controversial votes. If they concentrate their activities on serving their constituents through casework activities that have, in large measure, no policy content, they can largely immunize themselves from defeat. Not all House members choose this prudent, if timid, course, but it is available to them to an extent that it is not available to senators.

Senators, facing a daunting array of state interests, are often compelled to take stands that involve politically painful choices. They are prevented from adopting the strategy of merely conforming precisely to the interests of their constituencies because their constituencies are states, where it is unavoidable that there will be interests that will clash. They are also less able to take refuge behind friendly procedures in the Senate chamber. They can be forced to go on record with votes that are controversial and politically costly. In the House, procedures are so user friendly that members there can often appear to be on both sides of an issue.[29]

Some Senate elections contain implications for national policy that House elections have ceased to have. The 1980 Senate election made the Republicans the majority party for the first time in twenty-five years. In that chamber the stage was set for the vast economic changes of the Reagan era. The 1986 Senate elections, which returned the Democrats to the majority, virtually closed the door on any major domestic policy accomplishments for President Reagan in the last two years of his term, lost him a Supreme Court nominee, Robert Bork, and seemed to preclude any further military aid to the Contra rebels in Nicaragua.

While it would be extreme to argue that Senate elections are somehow more "national" than House elections because to do so would ignore such important factors as the quality of candidates and the importance of statewide issues, it has been possible to read national trends and moods into them more unambiguously than into House elections. In the same vein, it would be equally inaccurate to say that House elections have no national policy implications, but the very number of entrenched House members would make it difficult to achieve much of a swing in House elections.

To the extent that Senate elections are fought on the issues, they are, in a sense, more national. The attention lavished on them by the national media makes them so. The activities of contributors from beyond the borders of the state nationalize Senate elections. They have, accordingly, a kind of national quality not associated with House elections. House members can gain reelection by the successful advocacy and articulation of a limited set of interests; senators are called to account on a broader array of issues that embrace issues of concern to the nation as a whole.

But the difference in the electoral environments of House districts and whole states may have as much to do with the size of the legislative chamber to which the candidate belongs as to the number or variety of voters in the constituency. It is simply easier to find someone to hold accountable from the Senate than from the House when things go wrong. As political consultant Peter Fenn expressed it:

In the House there are 435 guys and, after all, one of them is my old friend Joe from down the street and I grew up with him and I'm not going to blame *him* that much for 20 percent interest rates, but you can bet your ass I'm going to blame that senator because he's only one of a hundred.

DO SENATORS TAKE THEIR ROLE SERIOUSLY?

In conversation with senators, the listener is left with the inescapable impression that they feel they deal with matters of greater weight and gravity than those who serve in the House and that speaking out on the great issues of the day comes with the territory of the United States Senate. South Dakota Democrat George McGovern expressed a view common among the older group of senators who began their congressional careers in the House.

Shortly after coming to the Senate, I made a series of speeches that were an examination of the contradictions in our kind of rigid fixation on Fidel Castro and I urged that we use Alliance for Progress [a program of economic aid to Latin America proposed by the Kennedy administration in 1961] not hostility toward Castro as the basis for our policy.

That was the kind of speech I felt comfortable with in the Senate. I guess I felt too much under the political gun to do it in the House. It wasn't that I was afraid to go on about things like that, but it was such a life-death struggle to save the farmers back home. The pressure of that one district problem was so intense that I was home every other weekend listening to it.

I was just so much more directly associated with the immediate concerns of my own district's problems than I was with the policies of the nation. Those things I found easier to examine in the Senate.

The level of issues the senator deals with is more apt to produce controversy than those locally oriented issues that seem to dominate House members' concerns. If senators see themselves—or are seen by the voters—as addressing the "big-ticket" issues, it is not surprising that they are held accountable for them. Some senators were adamant that senators should address these issues rather than take refuge in casework. As George McGovern put it, "If you don't talk about these things in the Senate, the system is not working the way it's supposed to."

The tendency of senators to become identified with national and international issues is a result of both preference and an institutional bias in the Senate in favor of large, visible, and often controversial issues.

The very breadth of senators' committee responsibilities contrasted with the relative narrowness of House members' substantive focus means that senators typically are called upon to speak out on a wider array of topics. In a sense, then, institutional imperatives force senators to be generalists whose views are solicited more frequently on a variety of topics, and these views are often newsworthy.

Constitutional distinctions such as those, for example, in treaty ratification confront senators with an area of controversy from which House members are exempted. Politically touchy treaties, such as the 1979 U.S.-Panama treaty that returned the canal to the Panamanians, present senators with a gauntlet that House members do not have to run.

The proportion of legislators assigned to the committees dealing with national security and foreign policy issues—perennially topics of great controversy—varies between the House and Senate. In the 99th Congress (1985–1986), for example,

almost 60 percent of the members of the Senate were assigned
to the following committees: the Appropriations Committee's
Subcommittee on Defense and Foreign Operations, the Armed
Services Committee, and the Foreign Relations Committee.
There are four parallel committees in the House, yet less than
25 percent of the membership of the House was assigned to
those committees dealing with international relations and national security. The stake of the Senate in these areas of public
policy is more than twice as large as that of the House. In a
sense, then, institutional imperatives combine with a sense of
being "senatorial" to direct senators into issues that are more
salient to the public and media and at the same time more
controversial.

The Senate's role as the institution that produces presidential possibilities also works to promote issue stands on the part
of senators. The toughness with which Senator Joseph R.
Biden, Jr., took on President Reagan's judicial nominees in
1987 and 1988 was intensified by his presidential ambitions. But
presidential quests that impel senators to take novel or radical
positions in order to cater to national party constituencies can
backfire on those who fail to get the nomination. They often end
up having to explain to the voters of their state why they took
such uncharacteristic positions. Going national and taking
stands that appealed to a national Democratic constituency
vastly more liberal than the electorates in their states was a
factor in the 1980 defeat of three prominent senators. George
McGovern of South Dakota became associated with opposition
to American foreign policy; Frank Church of Idaho exposed
excesses on the part of the CIA; and Birch Bayh of Indiana was
seen as an advocate of liberalized abortion policy.

Washington lobbyist Howard Paster, who served as Bayh's
chief legislative assistant, acknowledged that Bayh's 1976 bid
for the Democratic presidential nomination caused him to take
positions that put him at odds with Indiana voters, but argued
that even those senators without presidential ambitions take up
risky issues and causes.

Senators are more apt to play a role in cosmic issues that don't have a direct payback for their constituency. That sometimes can cause them either to neglect home or to be perceived to be detached from home and it can catch up with them in a political way.

But there is also evidence that the public expects senators to tackle big and important issues. A CBS/New York Times poll of a random sample of 1,254 adults, which coincided with the celebration of the 200th anniversary of the Constitution, found that 51 percent (as opposed to 35 percent) felt that the Senate was "likely to take a long-range view of issues" more than the House and, by a 54 to 29 percent margin, that the House "better represents the views of the people that elected them" than members of the Senate.[30]

Citizens, then, expect senators to be "senatorial"—more measured and less impulsive in judgment, less mechanistically tied to the specific views of their constituents. Americans appear not to want senators to act like House members. They are, however, not necessarily willing to reward that detachment and independence of mind with a long lease on the office.

HOW ISRAEL PLAYS IN ILLINOIS:
A HOUSE AND SENATE EXAMPLE

An impulse to embrace controversy can be costly to a senator, particularly if the issue on which he chooses to be bold or the forum in which he raises it is highly visible.

Charles Percy (R-Ill.) became chairman of the Senate Foreign Relations Committee in 1981 in his third term in the Senate. Considered something of a boy wonder for his leadership of the Bell and Howell Company in the 1960s, Percy was an adroit and successful politician who seemed headed for a fourth term in 1984.

Illinois is a complex state. With more than 11 million people, it is both intensely urban and resolutely rural. Extending from Lake Michigan to its borders with Kentucky and Missouri, it is both Northern and Southern.

Percy's 1984 challenger, Congressman Paul Simon, was an obscure but well-respected House member and was expected to fare no better than previous challengers to Percy because, despite Illinois' complexity, Percy had avoided association with any damaging issues. As one Washington lobbyist recalled, "Percy had always danced around issues very successfully. But he got caught up on one of those big issues and that could have spelled the difference between him and Simon right there."

The "big issue" was Percy's embrace of the leader of the Palestine Liberation Organization, Yassir Arafat, and his advocacy of a Palestinian state. Percy had never been a keen partisan of Israel, but upon assuming the chairmanship of the Foreign Relations Committee, he visited the Soviet Union where, in a conversation with Soviet officials leaked to the U.S. press, he expressed support for Arafat and a Palestinian state.

Percy's chairmanship of the Foreign Relations Committee magnified the news coverage given to his views on the Middle East. Statements by the chairman of the committee rank a probable third behind those of the president and secretary of state. No obscure or marginal commentator, Percy's views were given wide coverage in the media. The issue of Percy's stand on Middle East policy cost him reelection in 1984 as he lost to Simon by 2 percent (48 to 50 percent).

That was also the case in 1982 in the 20th Congressional District in Illinois where Representative Paul Findley, a Republican "who had done fine in elections as long as he concentrated on farm issues . . . became interested in the Middle East. He met Yassir Arafat and became convinced that the United States should accept many of the Palestine Liberation Organization's goals."[31]

While it is true that Findley, after twenty-two years in the House, was a senior member of the House Foreign Affairs Committee, the views of members of the minority party in the House do not have much resonance with the press on matters of foreign policy unless, of course, you proclaim yourself to be "Yassir Arafat's best friend in Congress." Findley's provocative claim was not as widely covered as Percy's, but it gave his Democratic challenger, Dick Durbin, enough of a boost to defeat Findley narrowly.

The difference between Percy and Findley is that the congressman literally courted controversy by the vocal and provocative nature of his stand on an issue not of central importance to a district interested mainly in farm problems. Percy, as chairman of the Senate Foreign Relations Committee, could not, by reason of the constitutionally distinctive jurisdiction of his committee, have evaded press attention on so controversial a topic as the Middle East. Findley expressed his views more flamboyantly and defiantly than Percy and suffered the same fate. The difference lies in the fact that Findley's defeat might have been averted had he not, in effect, stood in the middle of the road and asked to be run down. He might have continued to cast pro-Palestinian votes and even speak out for the PLO in the House, as more than a score of members routinely do, but identify himself primarily with the interests of his district. Percy's views could not be so easily disguised or finessed, and his defeat came more from the intrinsically controversial nature of the subject matter of a committee of which he was chairman and its place in a chamber to which foreign policy is an important—even exalted—topic.

If the issues with which senators are identified tend to be more national than those associated with House members, the sources of financial support for their campaigns are more national as well.

PACs and Deep Pockets:
The Financing of House and Senate Campaigns

The money to conduct congressional campaigns comes from three sources: contributions by individuals; contributions from state or national party organizations (such as the Democratic Congressional Campaign Committee for Democratic

House candidates or the Republican Senatorial Campaign
Committee for GOP Senate candidates); and contributions
from organizations known as political action committees
(PACs). Among PACs, the examples of most interest are multi-
candidate PACs. These are like political mutual funds in which
a donor who may not want to put all of his or her money in the
campaign of a single candidate will donate instead to a PAC
whose directors will decide where the contribution of that person and of thousands of others would be best directed. Some
PACs solicit funds to help liberal members, others to help
members and senators whose votes have helped the labor unions; still other PACs are set up by a single company to give
money to the campaigns of friendly members; the most powerful, the trade association PACs, are organized by entire industries as part of their lobbying activities. One example of lobbying activities by an industry is the National Cable Television
Association, which is based in Washington and to which all
local cable television companies belong. These companies'
membership dues in the trade association are based on the
number of cable subscribers they have, and the dues enable
NCTA to operate a PAC that targets money for the campaigns
of those who have been, or might be, friendly or influential on
matters relating to the industry.

While PACs have become more important since 1974 when
changes in the Federal Election Campaign Act made it easier
for PACs to raise and disperse money to candidates in federal
elections, it is still the individual contribution that is the most
important source of campaign funds for congressional elections
in both House and Senate races. There are, however, differences
in the sources of funds between House and Senate elections.

Senate candidates rely less on PAC money than do those
running for House seats. In contrast, Senate campaigns receive
a larger percentage of their funds from individuals than do
House candidates. In 1984, PACs accounted for 37 percent of
the receipts of House campaigns but only 19 percent of Senate
campaigns. In the same year, however, senators and their oppo-

nents were getting 65 percent of their money from individual contributors while House members and their rivals were receiving only 48 percent from individuals.[32]

Senate campaigns tend to draw more heavily than House campaigns on individual contributors for two reasons. First, Senate candidates—both incumbents and challengers—receive more publicity than their House counterparts and have a larger constituency geographically. According to Larry Sabato, this visibility of Senate candidates enables them to solicit money from individual contributors, especially through the use of direct mail advertising.[33]

The second reason is that fund-raising by direct mail is not practical in a House campaign. It is very expensive and the primary target of the mailing would be only a few hundred thousand households in the average congressional district. Given the relative anonymity of House members even within their own districts, it is unlikely that the representative's solicitation would elicit much of a response from a household halfway across the country. Yet this is one important way that money is raised by senators. Senators can use direct mail solicitation not only because they are so much better known—a Senator Ted Kennedy is as well known in Illinois as in his own home state of Massachusetts—but because their very visibility allows them to raise the money to invest in expensive mailings. Expenses such as mail solicitation are built into the large overhead costs of a senate campaign.

It is not only in the area of direct mail solicitation that the senator's financial scope is national. Washington lobbyist Howard Paster described the broader fund-raising environment of senators:

Unless the House member is the chairman of a big committee or some other bigshot, he can't fly out to Chicago or Miami or Los Angeles or St. Louis and raise money from individuals.

The fund-raising event in which individuals contribute to a congressional campaign by buying a ticket costing several hundred dollars or more is used differently by senators and House members. Unless the House member is a party leader or committee chair, the fund-raising event will be held either in Washington, D.C., or in the district itself. If the event is held in Washington it will be attended by lobbyists who have purchased the tickets. These lobbyists will normally represent interests that fall within the jurisdiction of the member's committee. Sometimes groups of members will hold joint fund-raisers. Groups of members will also drop in on events being held by their colleagues. The presence of several members adds to the drawing power of the event since ticket buyers will have more than one congressional hand to shake.

The senator's fund-raising universe is broader and more glittering. The visibility of senators gives them a celebrity value that enables them to tap the most affluent and politically aware individuals anywhere in the country. As one lobbyist observed, "Most House guys can't go to [socialite and party-giver] Mary Lasker's place on the Upper East Side for a fund-raiser. Almost any Democratic senator who really asks can get a fund-raiser at Mary Lasker's."

For the House member, the political action committee represents a very efficient way to raise money. Jay Berman, the Washington lobbyist for the recording industry, comments, "It's just very convenient when a new House member comes to Washington for him to identify some PACs, and their contributions will be the core of that guy's fund-raising."

From the PAC director's point of view, House members can offer a bigger return than can senators. For one thing, we have already observed the impressive ability of House incumbents to win reelection. PAC directors, not surprisingly, will direct contributions to the campaigns of those who will likely be voting in the next Congress on matters that concern the PAC. There is, accordingly, a heavy bias among PACs, in general, to incumbents of both parties. Although most PACs indicate that they show no preference as to whether their contributions go to House or Senate campaigns, those who do indicate a preference tend to favor the House and, within the House, the incumbent.[34]

While helping those most likely to be making policy contributes to the pro-incumbent, pro-House bias of PACs, there is also the fact that PACs can get "more bang for the buck" by giving contributions to a House campaign that may cost $500,000 to wage than by giving it to a $10 million Senate campaign in which the money is, in effect, "lost" among many other individual and PAC donations. Their money is more likely to be visible and appreciated by the House member waging the lower cost campaign, and it also helps those most likely to win. But influential senior House members with token opposition have taken to raising huge sums of money from contributors in order to scare away potential opponents. A $5,000 contribution by a PAC to one of these members would not stand out very distinctly.

PACs by their nature will always favor the most likely winners and support those in whose coffers the PAC coin will have the greatest luster: typically, incumbent House members. PACs with corporate or trade association connections will key their contributions to the member whose committee jurisdiction covers policies important to those industries. Senators or senatorial challengers do appear to be favored by one type of PAC—the one that represents a single large corporation. These company-connected PACs may have facilities in many states and the percentage of Senate elections to which they contribute will be high. They may also perceive a broader and more national perspective on the part of senators and find the very breadth of senators' committee assignments appealing.

Representation, Responsiveness, and the Two Forms of Democracy

Looking back on this chapter, we have seen that the electoral environments in which senators and House members operate are quite different. The intimacy and sense of being in control that characterize House members' relationships with their districts have few parallels in senators' relationships with their statewide constituencies.

House members may be sent to Washington by constituents with whom they can feel intimate, but their legislative decision-making occurs in a setting of little intimacy. As we saw in the previous chapter, it is the Senate that enables members to better interact on the one-to-one basis that promotes unitary democracy in Congress. "It is the means by which legislators come to perceive overlapping interests, to emphathize with colleagues and to recognize common principles—the means, in other words, by which they come to make decisions on the basis of common interests."[35]

There is a paradox to be found in the fact that House members are sent by constituents with whom they feel great closeness to represent them in a vast, anonymous, and often anomic House. Senators, by contrast, are delegated by sprawling, complex, and unknowable constituencies to interact in a highly personal way in a compact and intimate chamber.

The relationship between members of the House and their constituents influences profoundly the approach to legislation that they bring to Washington. In close, direct, and almost continuous contact with voters, House members hear the interests of those they represent expressed with great intensity. But even if House members did not stick so closely to their constituents, the greater simplicity of the average congressional district would still enable them to divine constituent interests far more readily than a senator can. But it is in the expression of those interests in their respective chambers that the differences in home state interactions and Capitol Hill interactions between senators and representatives become critical in whether adversary or unitary democracy emerges.

Indeed, in the very manner in which voters send House members and senators to Washington there is an expectation that House members will sail close to the prevailing winds of district interests; for senators there is an expectation that from time to time they will have the freedom to go off on a tack. The view among the senators I interviewed was that they saw themselves dealing with a broader array of issues and problems, and there was also a feeling among most of the senators that constituents, in the words of Senator Chris Dodd, "see senators as being involved in national issues. There's an expectation in peoples' minds. They may not understand the constitutional distinctions between a congressman and a senator when it comes to foreign policy but they sense that senators are supposed to be involved in that job." Though the rules of the Senate promote a kind of aggressive individualism associated with adversary democracy that puts senators in a better position to foster their constituents' interests, "senators, of course, can use their greater freedom . . . to raise broader issues."[36]

If, indeed, senators cast their debate and frame their concerns more in national terms, the Senate would appear to be the chamber where the values of unitary democracy are furthered. There was, however, a feeling among the senators interviewed that uncertainty about reelection was pushing senators into exaggerated defensive strategies of fund-raising that made them beholden to the very interests they were expected to stand above. Paradoxically, House members, for whom no broader vision is demanded, are reelected with inexorable regularity.

But even here, the higher electoral mortality of senators represents a greater responsiveness to national political trends. While House members can insulate and innoculate themselves from these trends by stressing service and dedication to the limited interests of the district, senators cannot usually do enough of these favors to make a difference. Sensing, albeit imperfectly, that Senate elections are the means to register sentiments about the trends of national policy and the course of the broader political system, voters unilaterally impose unitary standards of accountability on the upper chamber.

One strategy adopted by fearful Senate incumbents is to emulate the localism of House members by becoming what

New York senator Alfonse D'Amato calls "a pothole senator." While senators have long been free to choose from any number of representational styles, it may be more difficult for senators to restrict themselves only to noncontroversial activities. There is pressure both from colleagues and from voters that may impel even the most parochially minded senator toward a broader focus. These senators may still prefer to deal with potholes but, at the very least, they will be potholes on Interstate 95.

NOTES

1. Richard F. Fenno, Jr., *Homestyle* (Boston: Little Brown, 1978), p. 55.
2. Richard F. Fenno, Jr., *The United States Senate: A Bicameral Perspective* (Washington, D.C.: American Enterprise Institute, 1982), pp. 24–25.
3. Norris Cotton, *In the Senate* (New York: Dodd, Mead & Co., 1978), p. 51.
4. Ibid.
5. See Bruce E. Cain, "Assessing the Partisan Effects of Redistricting," *American Political Science Review,* 79 (1985), pp. 320–333.
6. Stephen Kemp Bailey, *Congress Makes a Law* (New York: Columbia University Press, 1950), pp. 126–127. The 17th District of Illinois currently embraces such industrial town as Rock Island and Peoria and is not nearly so rural as it was in 1950 when Bailey used it as an example of a district without much blue-collar influence.
7. Morris P. Fiorina, *Congress: Keystone of the Washington Establishment* (New Haven, Conn.: Yale University Press, 1977), p. 61.
8. Jacqueline Calmes, "House Incumbents Achieve Record Success Rate in 1986," *Congressional Quarterly Weekly Report,* November 15, 1986, p. 2891.
9. *Washington Post,* Friday, August 17, 1979.
10. Gary C. Jacobson, "Money in the 1980 and 1982 Congressional Elections," in Michael J. Malbin, ed., *Money and Politics in the United States* (Chatham, N.J.: Chatham House, 1984), pp. 52–54, and Gary C. Jacobson and Samuel Kernell, *Strategy and Choice in Congressional Elections,* 2d ed. (New Haven, Conn.: Yale University Press, 1983), p. 102.
11. Marjorie Randon Hershey, *Running for Office* (Chatham: N.J.: Chatham House, 1984), p. 166.
12. CBS/New York Times Poll, *Politics, 1986,* September–October 1986.
13. Thomas E. Mann and Raymond E. Wolfinger, "Candidates and Parties in Congressional Elections," *American Political Science Review,* 74 (September 1980), p. 626.
14. Ibid.
15. The two most influential works on the effective use of their incumbency by House members are: Fiorina, op. cit., who makes the simple point that the expansion of the scope of government—often at public demand—causes more citizens to get trapped in the toils of the federal bureaucracy and to turn to members of Congress to protect them from a government whose expansion they favored. Another picture is painted by David Mayhew in *Congress: The Electoral Connection* (New Haven, Conn.: Yale University Press, 1974), which points out that internal resources in the

House itself enable members to advertise their accomplishments to voters, claim credit for benefits they have brought to their districts, and take positions (often in the form of posturing) on issues that align them with the majority of the electorate. See also Bruce E. Cain, John A. Ferejohn, and Morris P. Fiorina, *The Personal Vote* (Cambridge: Harvard University Press, 1987).

16. Mann and Wolfinger, op. cit., p. 627.
17. Fiorina, op. cit., pp. 58–60.
18. James H. Kuklinski and Darrell M. West, "Economic Expectations and Voting Behavior in United States House and Senate Elections," *American Political Science Review,* 75 (June 1981), p. 438.
19. "Only 46% Can Name Congressional Representative," *Washington Post,* Sunday, August 1, 1982.
20. Alan I. Abramowitz, "A Comparison of Voting for U.S. Senator and Representative in 1978," *American Political Science Review,* 74 (September 1980), pp. 635–637.
21. Ibid.
22. Gary G. Jacobson and Samuel Kernell, *Strategy and Choice in Congressional Elections,* pp. 19–34.
23. R. W. Apple, Jr., "California Senate Race Reflects Electronic Era," *New York Times,* Sunday, October 19, 1986. See also Glenn R. Parker, "Interpreting Candidate Awareness in U.S. Congressional Elections," *Legislative Studies Quarterly,* 6 (May 1981), pp. 219–233.
24. Michael Barone and Grant Ujifusa, *The Almanac of American Politics, 1988* (Washington, D.C.: National Journal, 1987), pp. 825–827.
25. Bruce Lambert, "Silk Stocking District Sees Tough Congressional Race," *New York Times,* Monday, October 20, 1986.
26. Kuklinski and West, op. cit., pp. 436–447.
27. Ibid., p. 446.
28. The percentage of congressional staff assigned to work in state and district offices rather than in Washington has risen sharply for the Senate. In 1972, only 12.5 percent of Senate staff was in the states. A decade later it was almost 28 percent. House members, however, still assign a higher percentage of their staffs to district offices. For 1983, it was 36.6 percent. See Norman J. Ornstein et al., *Vital Statistics on Congress,* 1984–1985 ed. (Washington, D.C.: American Enterprise Institute, 1984), p. 123.
29. Mayhew, *Congress: The Electoral Connection.*
30. CBS/New York Times Poll, May 25, 1987.
31. Michael Barone and Grant Ujifusa, *The Almanac of American Politics, 1986* (Washington, D.C.: National Journal, 1985), p. 436.
32. Gary C. Jacobson, *The Politics of Congressional Elections,* 2d ed. (Boston: Little Brown, 1987), p. 63.
33. Larry J. Sabato, *PAC Power* (New York: W.W. Norton, 1985), pp. 74 and 77.
34. Ibid.
35. David J. Vogler and Sidney R. Waldman, *Congress and Democracy* (Washington, D.C.: CQ Press, 1985), p. 116.
36. Ibid., p. 87.

5

The Attentive Elites

Lobbyists and Journalists on
House-Senate Differences

APART FROM THE congressional establishment itself, which consists of the members and senators and their staffs, the two groups with whom legislators have the most direct and personal contact are journalists and lobbyists. They are the most important elements in the supporting cast of Congress. Their attentiveness to the institutions and the members as individuals is of such consequence that it is impossible to imagine the modern Congress without them. In the course of representing their clients' interests to Congress, lobbyists often become valuable personal friends of members and senators. Their presence in the legislative process—far from being intrusive—is probably indispensable. As purveyors of information, witnesses at hearings, suppliers of political resources, they are integral to the legislative process.

Journalists have a similarly symbiotic relationship with legislators. Without the comments and tape footage of members and senators, newspaper columns and TV news would be impossible. At the same time, it is the journalists—above all others—who tell the story of Congress and its members to the world.

In this chapter we will examine the relationships between these important supporting actors and the main cast of players, the legislators themselves. And we will look at those relationships in terms of the ways they appear in both the House and Senate.

The treatment accorded the House and Senate is not identical. Reporters and lobbyists see them in different ways, present themselves in different ways to members of each house, and emphasize different features of the two legislative bodies. Some lobbyists and journalists prefer to work the House; others indicate a preference for the Senate. Why this is the case is part of the subject of this chapter, but the relationship between the various news media and the two houses of Congress will receive first attention. What emerges is a very distinctive set of perceptions of the two legislative bodies on the part of reporters and lobbyists.

The Camera on Bicameralism:
Journalists and Congress

The lead story on NBC-TV's "Today" show the morning after the 1986 congressional elections was an unexpectedly strong showing by Democrats that enabled them to reclaim control of the U.S. Senate after six years as the minority party.

The first set of live interviews conducted by co-host Bryant Gumbel was with two senators and one member of the House: soon-to-be Senate minority leader Bob Dole; Senator Joseph Biden, a Delaware Democrat; and Representative Jack Kemp, a New York Republican. Kemp's involvement in the interview was not to solicit his views on the outcome of House elections—a result barely noted in the hubbub over the Senate—but to question him in his capacity as a Republican presidential hopeful for 1988. Indeed, the House races figured in only the most minor way in either the news coverage or the interview.

And why, indeed, should the House elections have merited more than tangential comment? An estimate by the *Congressional Quarterly* undertaken a week before the election showed that 340 of the 435 seats in the House were "safe" seats in which the incumbent or candidate of the party locally dominant was unbeatable. In the mere one-quarter of all House seats in which actual political competition was taking place, the struggles were being waged by incumbents who could be identified by only a minority of voters[1] and challengers whose visibility was so low that only 44 percent of voters typically reported even having had any contact with them.[2]

The next set of "Today" show interviews took place shortly after the 7:30 A.M. break to local stations. Two of the newly elected Democratic senators and the lone Republican who captured a previously held Democratic seat were interviewed. Still, no comment from a House member other than from aspiring presidential candidate Kemp. Just before the end of the first hour, however, mention was made of a specific House race when co-anchor Gumbel mentioned that of the two children of the late Senator Robert F. Kennedy who were seeking House seats, only Joseph P. Kennedy II, who was running for the Massachusetts seat once held by his uncle, John F. Kennedy, had prevailed. Apart from the bare reporting of the overall House results—a gain of six seats for the Democrats, the appearance of a presidential hopeful who just happened to hold a House seat, and a snippet of America's most intriguing political family—the fate of one of the two houses of the national legislature was barely mentioned.

At the beginning of the next hour, however, it appeared as if the House would finally be featured. Congressional correspondent Bob Kur, on the south side of the Capitol building, reported the overall results. He chose four individual House contests to expand upon. One was a contest in Iowa's 6th Congressional District in which Fred Grandy, the character known as "Gopher" on the TV series "The Loveboat," was elected. The second was in Georgia's 4th Congressional District where Democrat Ben Jones, who played the character "Cooter" in the TV car-chase series "The Dukes of Hazzard," was defeated by Republican Pat Swindall. Jones beat Swindall in a rematch in 1988 after Swindall was indicted for lying to a federal grand jury. The combination of celebrity and scandal made the 1988 race in the 4th District newsworthy again. Two other contests merited specific mention: Kentucky's 4th, where former Detroit and Philadelphia ace pitcher Jim Bunning had won as a Republican, and Maryland's 4th, where former Atlanta Hawks and Washington Capitols basketball star Tom McMillen was winning as a Democrat.

But the first half of the second hour of "Today" was not to be without its interview with a newly elected member of the House. The choice to represent the House was not Speaker-presumptive Jim Wright or even an up-and-coming back-bencher who had served a few terms. It was, rather, Joseph Kennedy II, who symbolized the coming of age of another political generation of Kennedys rather than anything notable about the House of Representatives itself. In the aftermath of the 1988 congressional elections, the young Kennedy again provided one of the few stories in the popular media about a House member. Representative Kennedy, reportedly "bored" with his work on the Banking Committee, had enlisted the aid of his uncle, Senator Edward M. Kennedy, to secure a seat on the House Appropriations Committee. This senatorial interference was promptly rebuffed and the appropriations seat went to Representative Chester Atkins (D-Mass.).[3]

So it is with the House and Senate. Senators who may possess little more than a certificate of election receive the attention that House members can earn only if they have an almost freakish quality. To be noticed in the Senate does not, to be sure, come about simply because you happen to be a senator, but to rise above the huddled and undifferentiated masses of the House may require traits that are less political than theatrical.

Richard F. Fenno has spoken of an "all-encompassing pro-senator bias on the part of the media."[4] While this verdict was meant to apply to the greater interest on the part of the local media in Senate campaigns over House campaigns, the same conclusion could be reached about coverage in Washington, although perhaps less categorically.

The percentage of legislators mentioned on the major networks' nightly news programs shows a pattern that consistently and heavily favors the Senate over the House. Data on the percentage of House and Senate members mentioned on these programs at least once in the course of a year were computed over a fourteen-year period beginning in 1969. In the average year over that period 89 percent of the total membership of the Senate would be mentioned at least on the nightly network news but only 37 percent of the House membership. The best year for the House was 1981 when 55 percent of its membership received at least one mention. That same year, 99 percent of all senators made an appearance on the news shows—the only uncovered senator being Hawaii Democrat Spark Matsunaga.[5]

One reason for a greater attentiveness to the work of the Senate on the part of the Capitol Hill press corps is already familiar to us: The size difference between the House and Senate favors the Senate. "It is easier and faster," Stephen Hess writes, "to build a coherent story with a smaller cast of characters. The House of Representatives is too much like *War and Peace;* the Senate is more on the scale of *Crime and Punishment.*"[6]

Factors that derive from the size of the legislative body seem to explain much of what journalists find fascinating in the Senate. One obvious appeal of the senator over a House member is that it requires fewer of them to stand out above the crowd. For one thing, the crowd is smaller, which means that journalists find it easier to get a sense of the identities of and relationships among 100 members rather than 435.

In practical terms, however, journalists are not even really dealing with a cast of 435 and a cast of 100. A compilation of the number of times senators were mentioned on network television evening news programs in 1981–1982 showed that roughly a half dozen senators were mentioned 100 or more times during the course of the year and another half dozen were mentioned three times or less. Indeed, the number of senators mentioned fifty or more times was only eighteen. That means that 72 percent of the membership was mentioned less than once a week.[7]

Christopher Matthews, press secretary to former Speaker Thomas P. O'Neill, made much the same observation about the House. "The House is like your senior year in high school," Matthews said. "You look in the yearbook and it's always the same people who are getting letters for track, starring in the school play, and getting elected to the National Honor Society. The rest of them are a bunch of nobodies."

Journalists also feel that the compactness of the Senate and the smaller cast of characters make it easier to sort out the players. Ann Compton, who covered the House for ABC television news, made this point:

It's easier to go after some identifiable name [to interview] and the Senate is just a smaller kettle of fish. It's easier to cover the jockeyings of a hundred members, but really you end up covering only thirty or forty. And that thirty or forty you really pay attention to on a regular basis consists primarily of chairmen and ranking minority members.

While stating a general preference for the manageability of the Senate for reporters, Compton raised an important qualification to the size advantage enjoyed by the Senate in the eyes of journalists: the number of definitive sources in the House may not be much larger than that in the Senate.

Linda Wertheimer, a congressional correspondent for National Public Radio, asserted flatly, "As a practical matter it's not any more difficult to cover the House than the Senate. In the House you need to know about fifty people well and sort of have an idea of who's who on an issue."

Journalists looking for a congressional spokesperson on an issue do appear to be drawn to those that can be identified as experts. "The national media need specialists; when they choose which senator to interview, it is often exactly because the senator can be counted on to be recognized as an expert."[8]

Stephen Hess established in his study of which senators receive the greatest media attention that journalists take the very logical step of going to those in the Senate whose leadership role or committee assignment gives them a plausible claim on expertise. But, as we have seen, the media appear to show a more generalized preference for senators over House members that seems not to be directly associated with expertise. Stated more bluntly, it is more likely that just any old senator will appear on the evening news than that any random House member will be interviewed. What does this generalized preference reflect? One possibility is that senators are deemed to be more knowledgeable and authoritative than House members.

But journalists uniformly indicated that on any given issue of public policy, it is a House member who is typically better informed as to the details and subtleties of legislation. One journalist who covers Capitol Hill for a radio network observed:

Well, you know, if you were going to talk about a health issue you would know that Henry Waxman [D-Cal.] would be able to tell you everything there is to tell about it. I don't know who you would talk to on the Senate side who would be similarly an expert.

When the observation was made to this journalist that former senator Russell Long of Louisiana was certainly an exception to this rule by virtue of his encyclopedic knowledge of the federal tax code that had no equal on the House side, the response was:

Yes, I suppose that Long was supposed to be the reigning expert but I always thought that it was because all the other senators were so poorly informed. With Long's expertise, I think, it was a case of "in the land of the blind, the one-eyed are kings."

IF SENATORS ARE MORE POORLY INFORMED
THAN HOUSE MEMBERS,
WHY DO JOURNALISTS LOVE THEM SO?

Considering first the conditions inside Congress that give rise to the media preference for senators, there is the manner in which the committee assignments systems of the House and Senate operate. As we've seen, the average House member is assigned to a single major committee while senators serve on three or more major committees. Any given senator, then, is better situated to speak out on a range of issues than is the typical House member because of the breadth and diversity of committee assignments in the Senate. If it is true that journalists seek out spokespersons who have at least the appearance of expertise, then one result would be that senators would be called upon by reporters more readily simply because the diversity of their committee assignments gives them some claim on familiarity in more areas. A good example of a senator being placed where a reporter is likely to want to reach would be Senator Edward Kennedy of Massachusetts, who serves on the Labor and Human Resources Committee, the Armed Services Committee, and the Judiciary Committee. Theoretically, then, he might be called upon in a single day to air his views on welfare reform, the performance characteristics of the M-1 tank, and a presidential nominee for the Supreme Court. In contrast, three of Kennedy's Massachusetts House colleagues serve only on their chamber's Appropriations Committee. Size again works in the Senate's favor on media coverage.

There is also the possibility, of course, that Senator Kennedy is being called upon to comment because he is Edward Kennedy—that it is his celebrity and visibility that are being sought as much as his expertise.

That possibility points to another characteristic of the Senate that causes its members to be more mediaworthy: those who come to the Senate with reputations already established in other fields.

People with established star quality in other professions have tended to run first for the Senate rather than the House. A glance at the 100th Congress reveals a considerable number of people whose renown antedates their Senate service and whose celebrity was helpful in winning one of the 100 seats in the smaller chamber.

Beginning at the "B"s with New Jersey Democrat Bill Bradley, one sees a former professional basketball player for whom the Senate was his first elective office. John Glenn, the

Ohio Democrat and first American to orbit the earth, is likewise a person whose political life began in the Senate. The same is true of Senator Edward Kennedy; Senator Daniel Patrick Moynihan, a renowned scholar, former sub-Cabinet official, and former U.N. ambassador; and John Warner, who is probably remembered less for being a secretary of the navy than for being the former husband of actress Elizabeth Taylor. The Senate, then, seems to attract stars. But it also has the capacity to make them. This is due, in large measure, to the fascination with senators on the part of the national media.

While he enjoyed a regional reputation as a talk-show host, North Carolina Republican Jesse Helms became the most prominent spokesman for ultra-conservative causes through his Senate service. Hess lists him as the fifth most-mentioned senator in the 1981–1982 period and puts Helms, Moynihan, and Kennedy in a category he designates as "originals"—"from the reporters' perspective they are the most fun to write about."[9]

Does the House have originals? It does, but not in such relative profusion. There is the irrepressible ranking minority member on the Appropriations Committee, Representative Silvio Conte, who once donned a plastic pig snout and ears to denounce pork-barrel politics in a floor speech. There is the bright, low-keyed Speaker, Tom Foley, and the burly and stolid chairman of the Ways and Means Committee, Democrat Dan Rostenkowski of Illinois, and the bright and acerbic John Dingell of Michigan, chairman of the Energy and Commerce Committee. As with the Senate, journalists of both the pencil and the camera turn to leaders and experts for their news stories.[10] The House, however, has so many formal leaders and experts that they outnumber the entire membership of the Senate.

There are roughly 150 committees and subcommittees in the House. While chairmen of full committees often chair one of its subcommittees, that still leaves more than 100 people who can call themselves "Mr. Chairman" or "Madame Chairwoman." Those 100 people do not even include the party leaders on both sides of the partisan aisle. Spokesmanship, then, is relatively devalued in the House in terms of both its profusion and its narrowness of focus compared to a Senate in which far fewer people with much broader responsibilities are available for interviews.

Among national reporters, particularly those associated with newspapers, the size difference comes down to a difference in access to the individual: House members are generally accessible to both print and electronic media. Senators will usually be automatically available only to correspondents from the major networks and granting an immediate interview to a reporter from even the most prestigious newspaper is not a foregone conclusion. Steven V. Roberts, who covered both the House and the Senate for the *New York Times,* contrasts the two chambers. Reflecting first on the prominence of staff—a factor we have already noted—Roberts says,

Senators have their Praetorian guard around them, squads of press secretaries. Sometimes, it takes two or three days to get an appointment with a senator. It takes about an hour to get an appointment with a House member if he doesn't actually pick up the phone immediately when you call.

In fact, part of the problem with the House is beating people off. You get calls from House members' press secretaries saying, "Don't you want to talk to my boss?" You get enough of them and you say, "All right, all right, I'll talk to your boss."

THE PRO-SENATE BIAS OF EDITORS AND PRODUCERS

It would be an unwarranted conclusion, however, to assert that reporters simply prefer senators over House members as spokespersons and subjects for interviews. Indeed, the preference that some print reporters show for the House hints at a more complicated explanation for the greater prominence of senators in the media, most notably in television news. The complication is that the TV reporters in front of the camera or behind the pencil are not the final word as to which story is broadcast or printed. Newspaper editors and television producers are normally the ultimate authority. Reporters from all

media insisted that the preference for Senate stories over House
stories among the member reporters was not clear cut, but that
among editors and producers, who decide which story the public will see, the senatorial story usually wins hands-down. Radio
reporter Linda Wertheimer reflected the opinion of the overwhelming majority of journalists interviewed when she asserted:

The Senate is more attractive to editors and producers, certainly. . . . In the House you don't have a lot of big-picture guys. Members
of the House don't wake up the morning after the election and understand that they are in the direct line of succession to the presidency,
as senators do.

Knowing that a story featuring a senator or with a Senate
dateline is more likely to appear on the evening news or on the
front page might well incline reporters to offer a senatorial story
to an editor or producer. This pressure is probably somewhat
greater on television reporters than on newspaper journalists. A
newspaperman argued that television reporters are aware of the
pro-Senate bias on the part of their producers and act accordingly.

The whole goal of TV network reporters is to get on TV yourself. Phil
Jones [congressional correspondent for CBS Evening News] wants to
be seen and say, "Hi, I'm Phil Jones," and at the end say, "This is
Phil Jones at the Senate." That's their bread and butter and deter-
mines their salary. If a producer likes Senate tape better than House
tape and you need to please the producer, you'll be inclined to do the
story with senators.

Among editorial decision-makers in journalism, then, there
is also a tendency to favor the Senate. While reporters may not
share in this preference, they appear to defer to it. In those news
organizations that assign one individual to cover the House and
another to cover the Senate, the Senate assignment is usually
clearly the more highly prized. Richard Benedetto of *USA
Today* stated flatly, "For a journalist to be transferred from

covering the House to covering the Senate would be regarded as a promotion in any news organization with which
I'm familiar."

DO PRINT REPORTERS LOVE THE HOUSE
WHILE CAMERA JOURNALISTS FAVOR THE SENATE?

Some journalists argue that print reporters favor the House
and television reporters prefer the Senate. This argument tends
to be made by print journalists, one of whom is Thomas Edsall
of the *Washington Post.*

House members are much more accessible to the print media. There's
a House lobby right behind the chamber and you can hang out there.
I used to find that you could get more of a feel for what was going
on just hanging out there. As the members came in to vote, you'd grab
the guy. They're much more casual than in the Senate. There is no
place in the Senate where only the press and members were allowed.
You'd have to go into the Mansfield Room adjacent to the chamber
with all the lobbyists and get a doorkeeper to go in there and get the
senator you want to talk to. And, of course, he's got to agree to come
out. It's a real pain.

Access to leaders is even more important than access to
rank-and-file members of the House and Senate from the journalists' point of view, and there was a distinct preference among
print journalists for the House style of leadership press conference over that of the Senate. One reporter for a major newspaper described the Speaker's lobby, which is located right off the
floor of the House, as "a wonderful meeting ground for members and reporters" and the Speaker's daily press conference as
"more useful than the Senate version, which gives you only a
truncated five minutes and then you're ushered off the Senate
floor and you can't follow up with questions."

Print journalists refer disparagingly to the majority leader's
press conference on the floor of the Senate as "dugout chat-
ter"—an abbreviated and unsatisfying mob scene in which reporters jostle each other to ask questions. Print reporters who

cover the Senate complain that although they are allotted fifteen minutes' time, the majority leader is usually late but de-
parts at the appointed moment. Steven Roberts of the *New York
Times* complained, "Usually you can only get in a few questions and then the bell goes off and you're immediately ushered
off the floor."

Charles Green of the Knight-Ridder papers points out that
one reason print reporters tend to favor the House is that
television cameras are not normally allowed in the Speaker's
lobby. This gives the press an advantage over television and
provides a kind of crossroads for journalists and members for
which no parallel exists in the Senate.

If print reporters like to cover the House, a survey of press
secretaries who work for House members indicates that they
prefer to talk to newspaper people more than they do to television correspondents. One reason for this is that it is simply
more difficult to get on television than to have a story written—
especially in a local paper. The same may also be true of Senate
secretaries for the same reason—a staff member such as a press
secretary might speak on behalf of a senator to a print reporter
and be quoted in a newspaper or news magazine as an authoritative source in the senator's office. Television reporters, however, want the actual senator and will rarely if ever use footage
of a staff member.[11] But the fact that their press secretaries
prefer to interact with print reporters is not the same as saying
that senators themselves choose print over television. They
make themselves available to television reporters in the Senate
TV gallery when a news story is breaking that might require
senatorial comment. Seated in front of what one television reporter called "the most famous row of books in America" in the
Senate's radio and TV gallery, those senators who have the
knack for the quick, pithy comment that comes across well on
a "sound bite" luxuriate in the national visibility they achieve.[12]

While print reporters praise the access and openness of the
House and its leaders, there appears to be no systematic difference as to which house is preferred by print and television

reporters that might enable us to say, for example, that print journalists favor the House and television reporters the Senate. The reason for this is an apparent distinction in the minds of journalists between the "play" a story receives and the professional satisfaction one receives. Reporters, as we have heard, want to file stories that are printed or broadcast and producers seem to favor Senate stories over House stories, all things being equal. Does this mean, however, that reporters necessarily favor the Senate? They are making a pragmatic judgment as to what is likely to get them on page one or a story on the evening news. Charles Green of Knight-Ridder reflected this set of calculations when he indicated a preference for covering the Senate in terms of getting stories published, "but in terms of having a more interesting assignment," said Green, "it would certainly be the House."

TELEVISION IN CONGRESS:
IS THE HOUSE'S MEDIA RIDE OVER?

The media advantage that the Senate had enjoyed in modern times seemed to be jeopardized in 1979 when the House authorized live coverage of its floor proceedings. While the number of people who became faithful viewers of the C-SPAN coverage of the House was not large, videotapes of speeches and debates began to be used extensively by the network news programs. Since there were no television cameras permitted on the floor of the Senate—the only television allowed being the occasional coverage of hearings—the House proceedings became the only game in town until 1986, when Senate television coverage began.

The immediate advantage enjoyed by the House in permitting coverage of floor proceedings can best be understood by reflecting on the fact that for more than 190 years the normal activities of Congress could only be learned of by the public after the fact. Here was a window on one house of Congress conducting its business for all to see. From the perspective of the television networks, moreover, the House was making it incredibly easy for them to get footage of Congress in action. By taping House proceedings from C-SPAN, there was an ample supply of fresh, vivid material available without having to dispatch correspondents or camera crews.

There is no question but that the House gained an immediate advantage over the Senate in the amount of broadcast-worthy material it was generating. The euphoria within the House was notable, perhaps even excessive. Former Speaker of the House Thomas P. "Tip" O'Neill boasted in his memoirs:

Thanks to television, the House of Representatives is now recognized as the dominant branch of Congress. In 1986, the Senate brought in TV cameras as well. But senators ramble on for hours, whereas our members can speak for only five minutes. . . . Now that the Senate is on television, the prestige of the House should continue to increase.[13]

The optimism of the former Speaker was understandable but probably unwarranted. Reporters are not attracted solely by the brevity or closely reasoned quality of a speech; they are also interested in who says it and how it is said. If editors and producers are convinced that something is said better by a senator because of the star qualities they associate with the Senate, then the Senate will continue to receive the bulk of attention from the media, particularly television.

There is a political factor that also needs to be considered in assessing the advantage the House has been said to have gained from the first use of television: The onset of the TV age in the House coincided closely with the political upheaval of 1980 which saw the White House fall to the Republicans and the Senate captured by that party for the first time in a quarter century. The House Democrats were, quite simply, the only Democratic game in town.

Where would a journalist turn for a Democratic opinion? Some turned to spokespersons from the Democratic National Committee, but most regarded the House as the locus of the loyal opposition in the years 1981 through 1986. By being

Democratic in a federal system dominated by the Republicans, the House received an institutional boost from journalists eager to ascertain Democratic positions.

The principal threat to the media hegemony of the Senate is the increase in the number of news-gathering organizations covering Congress. The development of satellite technology has enabled local TV stations that were formerly at the mercy of the networks to transmit their own coverage directly from Capitol Hill. More stations with the capacity to cover Congress means an escalation in the demand for spokespersons. With only 100 spokespersons, the Senate may not be able to provide TV producers with the high-profile senators they want for their sound bites and those producers may settle for the less luminous stars of the House.

The Legislative Stages: A View from the Lobby

While there is no accurate count of the number of people engaged in lobbying in Washington, more than 10,000 organizations have a presence in the nation's capital. Some of them occupy whole buildings or floors of buildings. Some operate out of small, crowded offices with volunteer staffs, and others may be represented by a single attorney in a large, prestigious law firm. The people who represent these groups may have representatives working on Capitol Hill almost continuously while Congress is in session; others may have all their lobbying accomplished in a single visit.

Organizations that lobby Congress fall into two large categories: membership organizations and nonmembership organizations. The first group contains "peak business associations" such as the National Association of Manufacturers and the U.S. Chamber of Commerce that are federations of thousands of member businesses and industries and advance the cause of business in the most general sense. Then there are trade associations that lobby for individual industries, from manufacturers of formaldehyde foam to the canners of tuna fish. There are labor unions, farm groups, and professional associations (such as the American Medical Association), as well as advocacy groups like the National Organization for Women. Nonmembership organizations consist primarily of individual corporations such as the Ford Motor Company, which maintains a large Washington office. But the nonmembership category would also include Stanford University and CBS.[14] There are also individuals such as the winemakers Ernest and Julio Gallo who hired a lobbyist to press for a provision in the 1986 tax reform law enabling them to keep the company in the family.

Some groups and individuals are represented by people known cynically as "hired guns," lawyers and public relations specialists who may be their sole Washington representatives or augment their permanent office staffs.

It can be taken as a general principle that the interests that lobbyists represent will determine, in large measure, who they deal with in Congress. Congress is specialized and so are lobbyists. Almost no one lobbies "Congress" on a routine basis. Most lobbyists, especially if they represent a single corporation or industry, will ultimately become familiar with one group of senators and members and their staff and know little about others.

A lobbyist who represents a big pharmaceutical firm may deal principally with the House Energy and Commerce Committee and the Senate Labor and Human Resources and Environment and Public Works Committees, and never have anything to do with the Armed Services Committees of either house or the two panels that deal with foreign relations. In contrast, the lobbyist for a pro-Israel group may be aware of the players on the House Judiciary Committee, but will certainly know a great deal about the House Foreign Affairs Committee and the Senate Foreign Relations Committee.

The differences between lobbying in the House and in the Senate are less obvious. On the basis of interviews with a dozen lobbyists, these differences come down to two factors that, as already noted, are closely associated: the distinctive constitutional responsibilities of each house, and the size difference that produces a very different set of internal rules and procedures for each chamber and affects the prominence of individual members, the degree of specialization in either chamber, and the role of staff members. It is not always easy to disentangle these two factors. The founding fathers, while they did not stipulate that the Senate be less than a quarter the size of the House, did envision a more compact chamber, and the Senate went on to adopt rules appropriate to that chamber's compactness.

But size alone does not define the difference. For example, the Constitution accords to the Senate exclusive authority to confirm presidential nominations of high governmental officials, including ambassadors, and vests in the Senate the sole power to advise and consent in the ratification of treaties. The framers wanted the Senate, as the body in which all states had equal representation, to be the repository of the pre-constitutional sovereignty of the states, albeit in a circumscribed form.[15] The Senate, accordingly, has normally been the principal antagonist to the president on foreign policy and the focus of attention in clashes over the conduct of U.S. diplomacy.

The difference between the House and Senate from the perspective of the dozen lobbyists interviewed could be summed up in two terms: size and scope. The size of the Senate is smaller and the scope of its members, by reason of their chamber's size and its constitutional role, is broader. The House is larger and the scope of its members, by reason of this larger size, is more narrow but also more well defined. From these differences in size and scope emerge five subsidiary distinctions that lobbyists make: (1) the big picture versus the small picture; (2) direct contact versus staff contact; (3) designer lobbying versus mass-market lobbying; (4) House champions versus Senate champions; and (5) predictability versus unpredictability.

BIG-PICTURE AND SMALL-PICTURE LOBBYING

When asking lobbyists about bicameral differences one must always bear in mind that many of them worked either as con-

gressional staff or even as members and senators before they
took up the lobbying trade. They have residual loyalties to their
old chamber and this tends to influence their views. Nonetheless, there appeared to be a general feeling among the lobbyists
that the level at which issues were discussed was loftier when
dealing with senators. Some lobbyists attributed it to the people
attracted to the Senate. As a lobbyist with a Senate background
now working in the foreign policy field said, "The policy-ori-
ented people come to the Senate."

What this means in practice for the lobbyist is that he or she
must make a presentation to a senator in terms that underscore
the broader implications of the issue they are pressing. A civil
rights lobbyist said, "When you want to persuade a senator to
do what you want him to do, most likely you are going to have
to argue in loftier terms than you would with a House member . . . what's in the national interest or what the profound
consequences of this legislation may be. In the House you get
into the nitty-gritty with more detail."

Supporting the argument that the big picture must be drawn
for senators but that technicalities are the stuff of dealings with
House members is the notion shared by several lobbyists that
senators disdain those of their colleagues who relish detail
work.

Some lobbyists confessed that they ask House members to
do things for them that they would be hesitant to request of a
senator. A member of a prominent Washington lobbying firm
enlisted the help of a House member to block an amendment
that would have been financially damaging to one of his clients.
"I don't think I would have asked a senator to do this. It was
a little bit esoteric."

Then, reflecting on what he would have done had this timely
intervention of his friendly House member not killed the
amendment, he mused: "I probably would have found a senator
and argued to him the broader public policy reasons as to why
the amendment was bad."

While it would probably be too strong to say that lobbyists
see certain activities as "senators-only" work and other catego-

ries as proper for House members, distinctions are made not only as to the kind of issue a senator might be better activated on and the issue better pushed by a member but as to the manner in which the same issue should be "pitched" to a senator or member. One gets the feeling in talking to lobbyists that certain technical or narrowly drawn issues are seen as "beneath" senators unless they can be ornamented with high-level implications.

I mentioned this senatorial association with high-level policy questions in the previous chapter on the House and Senate electoral environments and why senators seem more vulnerable politically. It appears that at least three sets of political actors associate senators more than members with the highest-level policy questions: voters, lobbyists, and, indeed, senators themselves. As George McGovern recalled: "You see it on the floor debates and in the committees. There are more appeals to history and less to the immediate claims and current passions."

Lobbyists interested in more parochial concerns or pressing issues not susceptible to appeals to the national interest tend to have less of a sense of this distinction. A lobbyist for a pharmaceutical firm told me:

OSHA [Occupational Safety and Health Administration] is a national issue. It applies to everybody. I let the [pharmaceutical trade association] or the U.S. Chamber of Commerce lobbyists deal with that. I'll tell a senator how many of our employees are in his state and localize the issue. So I don't deal in grand issues. I let other people do that.

What are the reasons most lobbyists who are in a position to do so aim their pitches to senators on a loftier trajectory? One reason supplied by lobbyists and senators alike is that senators have a perception of themselves as being more concerned with high-level policy questions and that lobbyists have learned to appeal to them on a level different from that used with House members. Representing states, senators are, *a fortiori,* more broad-gauged in their concerns than members, but the difference seems to be more one of kind than simply of degree.

Most lobbyists felt that senators were more immune from

petty political pressures and consequently independent-minded. The diversity of interests they represent renders them less vulnerable to the types of pressures that might intimidate a House member, according to this view. A lobbyist for a trade association observed, "It's a lot easier for a senator to say no to his real estate lobby. A senator is more likely to have people on both sides of an issue. They don't run so often and can balance off interests over a broader period of time."

This view is not shared by all lobbyists. A lobbyist with one of Washington's most influential firms felt that senators were much more subject to cross-pressures: "They've got to weigh the competing interests. You always want to tell the people you're lobbying what the downsides are, but if you're dealing with a senator from a major state, the chances of his having downsides are much greater." This was distinctly a minority position among lobbyists. Most would agree with Donald Matthews that while some lobbies in a senator's state can inflict mortal damage for a wrong vote, "Senate terms are long and constituencies large and heterogeneous [and] senators are seldom without discretion."[16]

Those lobbyists who saw senators as more insulated from pressure by reason of the diversity of interests in their states and the length of their term were the ones most likely to place their appeals to senators on a loftier plane. We have already seen evidence in Chapter 4 that the tendency of some senators to identify themselves with large and important issues may subject them to greater political peril than House members who emphasize service to constituents. Senators are also mindful that the larger statewide constituency encompasses a greater variety of interests and political challenges. But some, at least, appear to see the larger environment as a test of their political creativity and the Senate as a place to deal with issues of a more transcendent nature.

The overwhelming majority of lobbyists felt that senators had more political "wiggle room" than House members. Typical of the comments was one from the head of a trade association, who said, "House guys operate under a very narrow window politically." Another, the head lobbyist of a major industrial conglomerate, commented: "Senators act as brokers for a fairly diverse set of interests, but an awful lot of these House guys come from constituencies where they have to articulate a pretty narrow set of demands."

Aside from the two lobbyists who felt that senators were often more constrained politically because of the greater likelihood of conflict between different interests in their states, the consensus was that senators can be less parochial, more nationally minded, and, most significant from a lobbyist's perspective, bolder.

But there is another persuasive, if less noble, explanation for the more general and macropolitical appeals that lobbyists often feel they must employ with senators: Senators know less than House members.

More often than not they don't know what the hell you're talking about. Yeah, you need to talk in concepts—what's good for America—but I don't think that's because they have any deeper feelings for America than the guys in the House. I think it's just because they don't know the details as well. You can't talk to them any other way.

This assertion by a lobbyist for a major trade association is a variant of statements made by almost all of the lobbyists interviewed.

Some lobbyists have horror stories about the lack of specific knowledge that senators have of amendments that they themselves have introduced. One Washington representative of a trade association in the health field told of a meeting with a Republican senator from an eastern state. The senator's state was home to a large number of health product firms. The senator had introduced an amendment aimed at helping the elderly to secure low-cost medicines but the measure also contained a provision that the lobbyist saw as damaging to the industries he represented. The senator assured the lobbyist, "Look, I want to do what I can for the elderly on this amendment, but I certainly wouldn't want to do anything that's going to hurt your industry and I know there's nothing in my proposal that would do that." At that point, according to the lobbyist, the senator paused and looked imploringly at his staff and asked, "There's nothing like that in my amendment, is there?" Somewhat abashedly his administrative assistant said that there was indeed such a formula in the amendment that would impose restrictions on the industry.

Lobbyists were unanimous in asserting, however, that the fact that a senator was personally uninformed about the details of legislation—even one's own—did not imply that the senator could not quickly get the information from those who had it at their fingertips: the senator's staff. Senate staff enables senators to operate at a more cosmic policy level but also, by its very quality and abundance, forces them to be even more generalized and superficial in their grasp of policy.

DIRECT CONTACT VERSUS STAFF CONTACT

One area of House-Senate differences that every lobbyist cited was that personal contact with members was typical in dealing with the House. In the Senate, one-on-one meetings with senators were unusual. Lobbyist-staff encounters were the norm in the Senate and while most lobbyists' meetings on the House side were also with staff, there was a more routine and regular quality to lobbyists' contacts with House members.

One lobbyist reflected, "I had been a Senate denizen all my years of working on the Hill, but the ease of access to House members is one of those things that has come as a revelation to me. The general rule on the Senate side is that you usually have to be satisfied with seeing staff."

But lobbyists in general feel more confident dealing with Senate staff than with House staff. A lobbyist for a civil rights group said, "Senate staff really is in a way junior senators." Another lobbyist, this one from a major pharmaceutical firm, said, "Senate staff know pretty much what their bosses want.

They speak with a degree of authority. It's much more a mixed bag on the House side."

The lobbyists perceive Senate staff as having considerable authority. A lobbyist for a major trade association said bluntly, "If your arguments convince the Senate staffer, you've convinced the senator. You don't have to see him." Indeed, in terms of a lobbyist's negotiations with a congressional office, it is typically the case that agreements can, in effect, be clinched with Senate staff. The senator may be brought in at the penultimate stage for what is almost a formalistic or ceremonial meeting with the lobbyist if indeed a meeting is required at all. House members become personally involved at a much earlier stage and usually vest their staff with more restricted negotiating authority.

Lobbyists who represent corporations or trade associations identify a kind of protocol involving senators that is not widespread on the House side. It is a ritual akin to those we associate with international summit conferences, whereby extensive lower level staff work on both sides precedes a ceremonial signing of documents by presidents and prime ministers.

Senatorial summitry operates in the following fashion: Lobbyists make contacts with Senate offices to persuade the senator to sponsor or kill an amendment or bill, make a statement on the floor, help a lobbyist's client with the bureaucracy, or any one of a number of actions senators are called upon to perform. Negotiations proceed which, depending on the size and complexity of the lobbying group, may involve those people who work the Hill for an interest group. These lobbyists may not be the executives who head trade associations, or the senior partners in a law firm that lobbies, but often they too get involved personally.

When most of the detail work is disposed of by the Senate staff and their counterparts in the lobbying group, or if a problem develops with the senator, a new set of individuals enters the arena: the principals.

A lobbyist for a large industrial firm told me about his negotiations with the office of Edward M. Kennedy for the Massachusetts Democrat to introduce a bill of interest to the corporation. "The staff and I negotiated the bill," the lobbyist said. "Now that all the details are nailed down, we'll bring in Kennedy and [the CEO of the company] to shake hands."

Corporate and trade association lobbyists also agree with the blunt assessment made by a lobbyist for a trade association—you need a CEO to see a senator. What he meant was that if he needed to see a senator he would need someone of the stature of a chief executive officer of a corporation to underscore the importance of his concern. This does not mean that lobbyists, on their own, could not get access to the senator personally. Rather, it is that the deployment of a client who is deemed to be of equal rank to the senator is called for.

DESIGNER AND MASS-MARKET LOBBYING

Lobbyists will often work House members (other than key chairmen of committees) as part of a group; this is almost never done with senators—the latter receive individual attention. The "wholesale," "mass-market," lobbying of groups of House members and the "retail," or "designer," lobbying of senators as individuals are products of the smaller size of the Senate and the vastly greater amount of personal influence enjoyed by the individual.

The average member of the House can become influential in a variety of ways: by the consensus of those who serve with the member on a committee; by being an acknowledged power in a geographical bloc; by being an expert on House rules; or even by being a vote counter. All of these, however, involve getting large numbers of colleagues to line up behind you. Senators generally are seen as forces in their own right. Given the intense individualism in the Senate, it is unusual for senators to view themselves as part of a bloc. They do, however, look to colleagues to provide expertise, or political cover or innoculation on controversial issues. Sam Nunn of Georgia, for example, is the Senate's acknowledged expert on national defense, and there are few others like him in that body. In that capacity he not only gives informed judgments on military issues but can provide cover for a colleague who can point to the respected Georgia Democrat on a controversial issue and tell his constituents, "But Sam Nunn also voted for it." Nunn's expertise is strengthened by his role as chairman of the Armed Services Committee. In the House, though, there are so many more of these individuals whose influence extends beyond their own single vote.

As we have seen, moreover, House members are more apt to be part of social networks, sports groups, or informal sociolegislative groups than are senators. Lobbyists know that their jobs can be made somewhat easier by lobbying groups of members. Thomas A. Dine, director of the American-Israel Public Affairs Committee (AIPAC), the pro-Israel lobby in Washington, drew a distinction between the approach he takes with senators and the one he takes with House members.

The closest thing to a group of friends I know of in the Senate that's kind of intimate is [Jim] Sasser, [David] Pryor, [Dale] Bumpers, and [Don] Riegle. They sit together and they kid around a lot.

But in the House! This past week I was discussing strategy on the Foreign Aid Authorization Bill and some other matters at Larry Smith's house [Larry Smith, a House Democrat from Florida] and Larry had invited [Robert] Torricelli, Mel Levine, Gary Ackerman, Howard Berman, and myself and we all sat around and talked. That kind of discussion would never take place with senators.

I call on Howard Metzenbaum. I call on Bob Dole. One more thing—four members came to Larry Smith's house. No aides. If that meeting had taken place at a senator's home, if such a thing can be imagined, each one of them would have brought a staff person.

Lobbying in the House, then, would appear at first blush to be more cost effective. House members seem not to resent being dealt with in groups and the social dynamics of the House are conducive to group formation. But the picture is not so clear because of the size difference and the related differential in

influence between senators and House members. As one lobbyist described the process of developing support for a measure,
to achieve equivalence with a single senator "you've got to get
a group of congressmen. You need lots of bodies in the House,
but with five senators you've got a genuine national movement
going." A single senator straying off the reservation can cause
a lobbyist a bigger headache than the defection of a horde of
House members. AIPAC's Thomas Dine recalled one such
incident:

In 1984 there was an [anti-Israel] amendment by Nick Joe Rahall of
West Virginia. He had thirty votes.
    Since that vote I have not worried about that thirty. I know who
they are. I've dealt with all thirty of them. They would all probably
vote the same way again. But when we can get 390 votes, 410 votes,
that thirty doesn't cause me to lose sleep.
    But take the vote in October 1985 to delay the Jordan arms sale.
The vote was 97-1, I think. Chris Dodd [Democratic senator from
Connecticut] was that one vote and strictly on a procedural matter.
I've been all over him ever since.

    But Dine's issues are quite different from the vast majority
of those dealt with by most lobbyists. His are highly visible,
well-reported "big-ticket" items in a policy are where the Senate is regarded as preeminent. In like manner, every one of the
lobbyists I interviewed who represented a corporation or a
trade association spent at least some time lobbying the House
Ways and Means Committee because of its dominant role in tax
policy. These issues are usually highly technical.
    Key House members such as chairs of standing committees
can no more be lobbied *en masse* than senators, and the wholesale approach can only be used with relatively junior House
members. Independent lobbyist Harris Miller made the following point: "If I were dealing with any issue near John Dingell's
purview [John D. Dingell, D-Mich., chairman of the House
Energy and Commerce Committee], which I do with some of
the insurance issues, I'd ignore him at risk to my clients and

myself. On immigration, I have to pay as much attention to [Kentucky Democratic representative Romano L.] Mazzoli and [Texas Democratic representative Kika] DeLa Garza as I do to senators like [Vermont Democrat Patrick] Leahy, Kennedy, and Biden."

There are interesting exceptions to the use of the designer approach with senators and the mass-marketing approach with House members. Kenneth Duberstein, the White House lobbyist, recalled the 1982 tax bill, known by its acronym TEFRA (Tax Equity and Fiscal Responsibility Act), when House Republicans had deserted the White House and were not supporting the measure. Duberstein said, "It was going down the tubes and we lobbied that [in the House] as if it were a Senate vote. We went one-to-one. Most of the meetings the president had on TEFRA were bringing in the congressmen one-on-one to meet with the president. House Republicans—one-on-one— we used a Senate strategy to work in the House." The reason for this approach was the unusual closeness of the vote in the House.

So while the general approach used by lobbyists is to go after groups—generally small groups—in the House and to approach senators as individuals, there are circumstances under which a reversal of tactics is called for. Duberstein provided examples of the White House using group lobbying with senators when time was an element and the administration feared it would be barred from selling AWACs (airborne surveillance planes) to Saudi Arabia in 1981. "We took the Senate and lobbied it like the House," recalled Duberstein. "We went to groups—small groups of senators—and put them together."

While these exceptions are interesting and important, the norm described by all lobbyists is that of using the mass-marketing approach in the House and the designer style in the Senate, except in the case of House committee chairmen, who are given the same personal and undivided attention as senators. The nature of the issue being lobbied also dictates which approach is likely to be most effective. Tax issues find lobbyists

164	HOUSE AND SENATE

going one-on-one with House members as meticulously as senators would be lobbied on major presidential nominations requiring Senate approval or on issues in the foreign policy area.

HOUSE CHAMPIONS VERSUS SENATE CHAMPIONS:
WHO CARRIES YOUR WATER?

Lobbyists call upon House members and senators not only
to introduce, support, and kill bills and amendments but also
to champion their issues and even to rescue them. Is there any
general rule among lobbyists as to whether House members or
senators are more effective in "carrying water"?

Lobbyists found it somewhat easier to interest House members in taking on an issue because of the considerably greater
ease of access to these members. The House member is also
likely to ask more probing questions of the lobbyist because, as
we have seen, their grasp of the intricacies of issues is generally
better. For lobbyists, clearly, this can be a mixed blessing. And
the advantage in getting a well-informed hearing from a House
member is contrasted, by some lobbyists, with the greater
amount of influence enjoyed by individual senators. A civil
rights lobbyist noted, "If you can get a champion in the Senate
you have a much greater possibility of success than if you did
likewise in the House."

Most lobbyists felt uncomfortable making such a stark distinction on the question of whether to enlist a senator or House
member, and all asserted that their decisions would be dictated
by the nature of the issue involved. Nonetheless, a small majority of the lobbyists conceded that, all things being equal, they
would prefer to be championed by a senator.

The question of whether or not the House member is more
constrained than the senator in taking on an issue by virtue of
the member's smaller number of committee assignments is one
that divides the lobbyists fairly evenly. Jay Berman, president
of the Recording Industry Association, the trade association for
record companies, makes the case that senators have more
room to operate. "The senator can operate more effectively,"

says Berman, "because senators who want to be players and who have some jurisdictional responsibilities are going to have a greater opportunity to be players than House members who have comparable jurisdictional responsibilities."

Harris Miller takes a different view. "In the House," Miller says, "with its greater dispersion of influence, almost anybody can get involved. You'll find a lot of different places to do things in the House, but in the Senate, because of deference and simply because of time constraints, it makes more sense to leave it to the chairman. It's difficult to get someone in the Senate to take on an issue when it's not at all within their area of expertise."

It seems debatable, from the lobbyist's point of view, whether the greater influence of individual senators and their larger number of committee assignments would make them better issue champions than House members with their greater ability to take on and comprehend new issues. The individual senator certainly looms larger in the Senate than the average House member does in the House, but the senator is also strapped for time to concentrate on an issue, much less to expend the resources to take a lead on it.

Some recent research indicates that the breadth of Senate committee assignments and the lack of constraint that comes with membership on those panels enable senators to use their committees as bases to champion issues more than is the case with House members and their committees. But at the same time, senators are picking and choosing more and more among issues on which they are willing to take a leadership role. In many instances they are passing on their discarded issues to House members from their state.[17]

While tactical subtleties abound, it does seem that there is a fairly clear set of advantages and disadvantages to using either a senator or a House member to take a leadership role on an issue or even to embrace it in a less conspicuous way. The calculation might run something like this for the lobbyist: A senator is less likely than a House member to take up my cause but in the more remote event that the senator does agree to

champion my issue, the vastly greater amount of personal influence and public visibility that senators can draw on can, in
competent hands, produce desired results.

A civil rights lobbyist interviewed in 1986 before the Democrats recaptured the Senate from the Republicans mused on
who would be best to take up the issues he cared about.

The Senate clearly gets more attention from the media and the spot-
light is more usually focused on individual senators and the Senate as
a body, therefore you might want the Senate as a platform, but for the
last six years you have the Democrats and most of your champions
controlling the House and they control the committees and subcommittees and the hearings.

But the civil rights lobbyist conceded that for the kinds of
issues that he pressed, the Senate was the place to go. He shared
this preference with the other "cause" lobbyists. These lobbyists for nonprofit organizations that are concerned with issues
ranging from the Middle East to the environment to civil rights
said that issues with national implications, as opposed to more
detailed and technical legislation, were best pursued in the
Senate. They seemed to feel that senators warm to these issues
and that the media warm to senators. If you can infuse one of
the senators with passion for your cause and convince him or
her that great policy consequences can be read in it, the senator
can be an estimable catalyst and attract national attention.

WHICH HOUSE IS MORE PREDICTABLE?— THE VERDICT OF THE LOBBYISTS

Most lobbyists deal with a fairly constant set of players—
both members and staff—on Capitol Hill. Much lobbying,
moreover, takes place within the context of policy "subgovern-
ments"—relatively small groups of lobbyists, members, staff,
and bureaucrats who combine to routinely make policy in specialized and noncontroversial areas of which the press and
public are generally oblivious.[18] The relationships between lobbyists for a particular industry or large corporation and mem-

bers and senators whose states and districts are home to those interests are remarkably stable. A lobbyist for a firm in the entertainment business in Hollywood said, "If somebody is trying to stick it to us on the Appropriations Committee, we have a California guy on that committee. We have a California guy on Energy and Commerce and a California guy on Ways and Means." Lobbyists who represent a broad and changing group of clients find that their cast of characters is more varied, but even they work through members they already know to get access to members they know less well.

Even in this relatively stable environment, unpleasant surprises come up. Like the old adage of navy pilots that flying off a carrier is hours of boredom punctuated by moments of terror, even the orderly life of a lobbyist can be rocked by the unexpected. Where is the unexpected most likely to take place? The lobbyists interviewed came down squarely on the side of the Senate as the body with the most surprises.

And we have already observed the power of the individual senator to "break all the toys in the sandbox," to use John Culver's expression, meaning that leadership is less able to guide the Senate according to the kind of timetable that House leaders have come to rely on. A man who lobbies insurance interests reflected, "At the end of every year, there is a series of articles in the newspapers about how [former Senate Majority Leader Robert C.] Byrd really had things under control and moving right along, brought his Defense Authorization Bill up in May or late April and then the world crashed in around his ears. Yes, I'd say the Senate is more unpredictable."

Someone who lobbies on a much different issue—civil rights—had much the same assessment: "One person in the Senate can foul things up whether it's in the committee or on the floor. That's much harder to do on the House side. It's difficult to prepare adequately for a Senate lobbying campaign, to plan a strict timetable. You can come up with a relatively strict timetable that you'll meet most of the time in the House, but you have to give the Senate a lot of leeway." So important a problem for senators is the chamber's unpredictability that a pledge to impose discipline on the schedule was a major factor in the victory of Senator George Mitchell of Maine in the race for majority leader in 1988.

Issues, Interests, and Complexity in the Two Houses

Journalists and lobbyists, as we have seen, approach the House and Senate with somewhat different expectations of the two chambers and its members. From journalists—most notably newspaper editors and TV news producers—there is an expectation that senators are able to address themselves to a broader array of issues and somehow see the larger picture. Most lobbyists see senators as enjoying a latitude in their actions and being able to balance off interests in such a way as to allow more flexibility than that permitted House members. Lobbyists certainly appear to frame their appeals differently to those in the Senate and those in the House. At least some of this more general scope with its direct or indirect message of national implications may be a product of the need to adjust to senators' imperfect knowledge of details. However, some lobbyists do find that invoking the general good on the Senate side is at least a useful way to get the attention of a senator.

It is a tantalizing question whether the pursuit of an interest is best pressed in the House or the Senate. While a great deal of that calculation, from a lobbyist's point of view, would have to do with such things as the nature of the issue, the quality of personal ties to a member or senator, or any number of other factors having to do with committee jurisdiction, it may be that some *kinds* of issues fare better in the Senate and other kinds fare better in the House for reasons stemming from the very nature of the two bodies.

Without question, the great flexibility of the decision-making process in the Senate puts senators "in a better position to

further constituents' interests than representatives are. This too
strengthens adversary democracy in the Senate relative to the
House."[19] Senate rules enable a senator to take up an issue at
almost any point in the legislative process and force consideration of it by the entire membership. The senator, moreover,
need have no association with the committee that would have
jurisdiction over the issue. The House, with its Rules Committee acting as an arm of leadership and more of a determination
role taken by committees, offers fewer opportunities for just any
representative to champion just any issue.

But would a senator be the person to turn to if a lobbyist
wanted a champion for a relatively minor issue or one with
strictly local implications or one that affected few people?
Given the size and complexity of their constituencies, the dif-
fuseness of their committee responsibilities, and the image that
they and others have of their proper role, a senator would
probably not be the one to enlist to champion a highly localized
issue affecting few people. The openness of the legislative process in the Senate certainly makes it easier for any given issue
to be considered, but, as we have seen, senators do not promote
any given issue. Indeed, "senators are most likely to use their
influence on behalf of those with the resources to communicate
their interests most strongly."[20]

While all senators are equal, all issues clearly are not equal.
The Senate, accordingly, is probably a poor place to press issues
that senators would regard as too narrow or too limited. But
don't such issues deserve to be heard and considered? Is it not
important that there be a place in the federal system that is
receptive to issues that may affect few people or are essentially
local in nature? One of the most thoughtful observers of Congress, former representative Richard Bolling of Missouri, de-
clared, "The House is the only place that the little interests get
heard." One might go even further and say that in the House
all issues are created equal.

What seems to emerge is a picture of a Senate whose procedures promote the consideration of some kinds of interests. So

while the Senate may be said to be adversary in its procedures in that it is a relatively open field for the championing of interests and issues at almost any point in the legislative process, the scope and substance of the interest seem to have an influence on whether or not senators will take it up. The tendency of the Senate to deal in larger aggregates than the House suggests that the Senate, while adversary in process, is unitary in outcome. The House, with its greater control over the legislative process by party leaders, is procedurally unitary. Its receptivity to small issues and its tendency to frame legislation that takes account of a myriad of small interests make it adversary in outcome. Every member of the House is assumed to have one or more interests sacred to their district and these interests are respected by all, because all House members have them. The legislative work products of the House bear the marks of this fragmentation.

NOTES

1. George Gallup, "Only 46% Can Name Congressional Representatives," *Washington Post,* Sunday, August 1, 1982.
2. Alan I. Abramowitz, "A Comparison of Voting for U.S. Senator and Representative in 1978," *American Political Science Review,* 74 (September 1980), pp. 633–640.
3. *New York Times,* Wednesday, December 7, 1988.
4. Fenno, *The United States Senate,* p. 11.
5. Timothy E. Cook, "Newsmakers, Lawmakers and Leaders: Who Get on the Network News from Congress," paper presented at the annual meeting of the American Political Science Association, Washington, D.C., August 30–September 2, 1984, pp. 9–11.
6. Stephen Hess, *The Ultimate Insiders* (Washington, D.C.: The Brookings Institution, 1986), p. 91.
7. Ibid., p. 136.
8. Ibid., p. 37.
9. Stephen Hess, "Being Newsworthy," *Society,* 24 (Jan./Feb., 1987), p. 39.
10. Cook, op. cit., pp. 13–17.
11. Stephen Hess, "A Note on Senate Press Secretaries and Media Strategies," Brookings Discussion Papers in Governmental Studies (Washington, D.C.: The Brookings Institution, April 1987), pp. 18–19.
12. Larry Warren, "The Other Side of the Camera: A TV Reporter's Stint as a Congressional Aide," *PS,* 19 (Winter 1986), pp. 43–48.
13. Thomas P. O'Neill, with William Novak, *Man of the House* (New York: Random House, 1987), p. 290.
14. These categories are provided in Kay Lehman Schlozman and John T. Tierney,

Organized Interests and American Democracy (New York: Harper and Row, 1986), pp. 38–51.

15. *The Federalist,* #62.

16. Donald R. Matthews, *U.S. Senators and Their World* (New York: Random House, 1960), p. 188.

17. Steven S. Smith, "Informal Leadership in the Senate: Opportunities, Resources, and Motivations," paper prepared for the Project on Congressional Leadership of the Everett McKinley Dirksen Congressional Center and the Congressional Research Service, September 30, 1987, pp. 4–10.

18. See Randall B. Ripley and Grace A. Franklin, *Congress, The Bureaucracy, and Public Policy,* 4th ed. (Chicago: Dorsey Press, 1987), pp. 6–10.

19. Vogler and Waldman, *Congress and Democracy,* p. 87.

20. Ibid.

6

Convergence, Divergence, and Persistence

Are the House and Senate Becoming More Alike?

"IN EVERY RESPECT 'Their High Mightiness, the Senate,' attracted less attention than the younger, popularly elected members of the House. . . . Although the ladies were permitted to sit on the Senate floor, and were restricted in the House to the galleries, they found their favorite orators in the lower chamber. 'Over in the House members have a great propensity to speak to the galleries and for the newspapers . . .'"[1] These observations on House-Senate differences made in the early years of the nineteenth century strike us as inconsistent with what we have learned about the characteristics of the two chambers from Chapters 2 through 5. We hear of a House esteemed for its oratory and its members making remarks in the hopes of being quoted by journalists while the "national gray-beards" of the Senate "hold all wit and humor in abomination" and conduct "somniferous debates" before resolving "not to expend a few dollars."[2]

Despite the distinctive roles granted to the House and Senate by the Constitution, the characteristics of the two and their relationships to each other are not static, as we saw in Chapter 1. The House, which was less than three times the size of the Senate in 1789, is now more than four times its size, the ceiling of 435 having been imposed by statute in 1911. Three years later the Seventeenth Amendment was ratified giving the people the right to elect U.S. senators directly and stripping the state legislatures of the function. During World War I, the first limitation on debate in the Senate since the earliest days of the institution was imposed, Rule 22. It was modified in 1975 to ease somewhat the ability to muster a vote of cloture to limit the filibuster. The House authorized the televising of its floor debates in 1979 and seven years later the Senate duplicated the action. This recitation of just a few of the changes over the course of 200 years is meant only to suggest that relationships we think of as fixed and established are subject to alterations either by formal action or by custom and usage. The very committees that seem today such a natural component of a legislative body have no documentary basis in the Constitution any more than do political action committees or the practice of having the House initiate appropriations bills.

Changes in the institutional personalities of the two bodies can also take place over a much shorter time period than two centuries. Accordingly, it could be said in 1970, "The essence of the Senate is that it is a great forum, an echo chamber, a publicity machine. Thus 'passing bills,' which is central to the life of the House, is peripheral to the Senate."[3] Only sixteen years later, the appraisal was different: "There is unprecedented opportunity for individual [House] members to present themselves as analysts, commentators, polemicists, and specialists in quick reaction to events around the world."[4]

As for the House being an efficient legislative machine, in the era of budgetary constraints there has been little in the way of raw materials for the machine to process. The legislative agenda in terms of really important measures has been curtailed so drastically by budget-balancing requirements such as the Gramm-Rudman-Hollings law that House members talk of a "four-bill" session in which action is virtually limited to four pieces of "must-pass" legislation: a couple of budget bills, a debt-limit extension, and some appropriations bills. It is a system that involves very few members and frees the rest to pursue symbolic activities and constituent-oriented duties that solidify their ties to the voters and the interests they work to cultivate.[5]

Thus the behavior of members adapts to alterations in the way the legislative system operates, but the legislative system also responds to changes in members and their objectives. The House was changed profoundly by a reform movement that began in the late 1960s and reached its zenith after the election of the House class of 1974—a group of younger Democrats elected in reaction to the Watergate scandal. It was a movement whose magnitude had no parallel in the Senate. By the time this reform surge had spent its force, the institution had been changed profoundly. Power that had been held by two groups of senior members—party leaders such as the Speaker and roughly twenty chairmen of standing committees—was more broadly dispersed. Subcommittees, which had existed only at the sufferance of the chairmen of standing committees, were institutionalized. By the simple reform of the committee system, more House members were able to refer to themselves as "Mr. Chairman" or "Madame Chairwoman" and to participate actively in the legislative process. Those reforms and others made the House a different place, but they did not necessarily make it more like the Senate.

There has been a tendency to seize upon some changes whose long-term effects are by no means certain and suggest that they represent, or at least presage, vast and permanent changes in the essential character of the House and Senate with the cumulative effort of making them more alike. The advent of television, as we saw in the previous chapter, was proclaimed by no less a figure than the Speaker as evidence of the future dominance of the House. It seems at least as likely that the unique place occupied by the Democratic-run House in years of Republican dominance in the White House and Senate aided the new visibility of the chamber and that the introduction of TV into the Senate in 1986 pretty much eliminated the House's temporary advantage.

There is no mistaking the fact that a House with more centers of power gives more people estimable perches from which to offer themselves as experts. As we have seen, journalists turn for comment to those who have an appearance of authority and expertise. There are certainly more voices in the House now with that kind of resonance. When this abundance of authoritative voices is coupled with an explosion in the number of television stations with personnel in Washington to cover Congress, we do seem to be hearing more from the House and seeing the faces of more House members. Does this mean that the House is becoming more like the Senate or that the House is becoming different from the way it used to be?

The purpose of this chapter is to examine the proposition that changes in both chambers and their political environments in recent years have caused them to converge. Almost no one says that they have become more distinct, one from the other. But there is an important third position—while some House members have come to act like senators in some areas and some senators have begun to assume characteristics of House members in some areas, important differences persist. These differences are of such a fundamental nature as to make the apparent points of convergence—or at least the scope of duration of that convergence—open to question.

The Case for Convergence

Scholars and journalists who see the House and Senate becoming more alike cite a number of examples to substantiate their claim. Viewed broadly, the points of convergence relate to the following: procedures; interpersonal and institutional loyalties; campaigning behavior; policy expertise; and the value of leadership positions.

Those who make the case for convergence find evidence for the following:

1. The House has suffered a decline in the efficiency of its legislative process and has become a more unpredictable body in the manner of the Senate.

2. A heavier Senate workload and an increase in the num-

bers and the attendant rise of influence of staff have caused a
deterioration in the interpersonal comity and accommodation
that has long defined the Senate. This is associated with a
decline of institutional loyalty, disillusionment, and a more
rapid turnover of members and seems to point to more chances
for stardom in the House.

3. Senators are beginning to experience greater electoral
insecurity and to act more like House members by campaigning
almost constantly for six years, as the House members do for
the two years of their incumbency.

4. Senators are actually becoming more engrossed in the
minutiae of legislation and House members are acting like generalists—an apparently dramatic role reversal.

5. The value of leadership positions in the House—both
party and committee—has diminished, and the hierarchy of the
House has become more flattened to resemble that of the Senate
where power is more evenly distributed.[6]

Let us look first at the question of changes in the legislative
process in both chambers. The case was made by Norman
Ornstein in 1981 that the control over the legislative process
exerted by the formal leaders of the House had been eroded by
the dispersion of power to the many new centers of power in
the subcommittee, producing "an ad hoc institution without
firm control over its own schedule or priorities—much like the
Senate."[7]

THE HOUSE: UP FROM ANARCHY

One expression of the enfeebled grasp of the Speaker and his
lieutenants was that "the House floor is often a free-for-all,
rarely a ratification point for decisions pre-structured by one or
two specialists."[8] While Ornstein's observation more accurately
describes the time at which it was made, what he may actually
have observed was a House in a state of flux due to temporary
forces.

The early 1980s were indeed a period of uncertain leadership in the House. The Democrats were demoralized by the

decline in the fortunes of the Carter administration and its ultimate defeat by Ronald Reagan. In the 1981–1983 period, Speaker Thomas "Tip" O'Neill had lost effective control of the House even though the Democrats enjoyed a numerical majority. The most consistent policymaking force in the House was a combination of House Republicans, who were remarkably cohesive in their support for Reagan administration policies, and a group of Sunbelt Democrats, the so-called "Boll Weevils," who voted with the GOP members on such crucial issues as budget-cutting and tax-cutting legislation.

The situation changed abruptly after the election of 1982 with a twenty-six-seat gain by Democrats in the House that eliminated much of the influence of the Boll Weevil Democrats. Few of these new Democrats became affiliated with the Boll Weevils. Even the humiliating loss by Walter Mondale to President Reagan in 1984 did not materially affect Democratic strength in the House.

Far from being a free-for-all, the end of the O'Neill years saw House leadership with its hand firmly on the wheel. So effective did this control appear to be that Alan Ehrenhalt could write in 1986, "The O'Neill years have seen the floor evolve into a much more efficient legislative machine, with most major bills brought there under procedures barring more than a handful of amendments. . . . House leaders and the Rules Committee have kept the terms of debate and amendment under tight control."[9]

Phenomena such as the temporary loss of control by the Speaker are important but tend to be the products of short-run forces. But can it be said that the firm control now in the hands of House leaders may be as transient as the free-for-all of the early 1980s? Possibly. But it is more likely that the House is, by its very nature, an institution that needs a strong guiding hand and that no one appreciates this fact more than the members themselves. Senator Richard Schweiker said it simply in 1986: "The House is still autocratic and the Senate is in chaos. I don't think that's really changing."

The laissez-faire atmosphere in the House that was discerned in the early 1980s as evidence of a House becoming more like the Senate has also been a victim of the "four-bill system." The unavailability of money for new programs means, among other things, that only those committees with jurisdiction over "must-pass" bills are going to be full participants in the process. The main centers of activity in the House are the Budget Committee, with its responsibility for the budget resolution and reconciliation bills; the Appropriations Committee, with its jurisdiction over the thirteen appropriations bills (or the continuing resolution that is passed in the absence of them) and supplemental appropriations bills to augment money already appropriated to any agency or program; Ways and Means, because of its jurisdiction over tax matters; and Energy and Commerce, a kind of supercommittee with such a broad jurisdiction that even during lean times it has a great deal to do.

If the processing and passage of bills is the measure by which we judge a well-functioning House, relatively few players are involved in the key legislation, and what measures are enacted bear the strong imprint of committee and party leaders. Far from being a free-for-all, the contemporary House is like a vast bridge tournament with a few players and scores of kibitzers.

Indeed, it is the activity of kibitzing to which many of the excluded members turn in a Congress with so little legislative action. Committees that process only one piece of legislation in a year, such as the House Foreign Affairs Committee, have little to offer their members other than a platform for media appearances. Members such as New York Democrat Steven Solarz— referred to snidely as the Foreign Minister of the House—have used the Foreign Affairs Committee to great advantage to publicize the issues with which they are involved.

THE SENATE: A RETURN TO CHAOS, COURTLINESS, AND COMITY

The Senate, in contrast, seemed in danger of turning into a well-regimented clone of the House in the early 1980s. "The

Senate," Ornstein wrote, "has become *more* formal and impersonal, *more* tightly organized through its 'reformed' committee system, and developed *more* rigid floor rules and procedures."[10] By the first session of the 99th Congress in 1985, Senator Thomas Eagleton, a Democrat of Missouri, was rising on the floor to proclaim the Senate to be "in a state of incipient anarchy." Eagleton's Missouri colleague, Senator John Danforth, a Republican, had only one quarrel with Eagleton's characterization of the Senate. He suggested deletion of the modifier "incipient" and substituting for it the phrase "fully developed." What anarchy means, Danforth reminded his colleague, is "everyone is a law unto himself."[11]

It is important to look back again to the early 1980s and remark that although the observations about a more docile and tractable Senate were probably accurate at the time they were made, the Senate is by nature such an individualistic body that such periods do not last long.

The use of the filibuster, which seemed to be coming under tighter control in the late 1970s, is now used or threatened as a device to block consideration of legislation with considerable abandon. While the termination of the filibuster has become somewhat easier, it is still an effective enough tactic that even the mere threat by a senator that he or she will filibuster a bill will often cause the leaders to shelve the measure. No longer used exclusively to block action on civil rights bills by willful segregationists or even as a device to protect the interests of small states, the filibuster is now used, according to Senator Charles Grassley, for "piddly little issues." Arizona Democrat Dennis DeConcini sees its capricious use as a "disservice to the institution and to the orderly consideration of issues here."[12]

The image of a more docile Senate and a more unruly House seems to have been a transitory phenomenon. Contemporary observers see the House as an orderly and mostly predictable place and the Senate as a thicket of unexpected snares and pitfalls.

The evolution of the Senate into a place of anonymous

members who offer little to one another in the way of comity
or friendship and the emergence of House members who stand
out by reason of their individual qualities also bear examination
as an indicator of convergence.

A decline in the quality and quantity of interpersonal relationships in the Senate, if it could be documented, would constitute a profound change in the institution. Recalling Chapters
2 and 3 and the discussion of the powerful effect of chamber size
on the way business is conducted in the two houses, the elabo-
rateness of House rules and the simplicity and brevity of Senate
rules mean much is left to personal negotiation in the Senate
between members of that body. The rise in importance of staff
as intermediaries between overworked and overcommitted
senators has already been noted. It is almost unheard-of to be
able to talk to a senator for more than a few minutes without
hearing complaints about the workload or about the increased
importance of staff. Neither of these changes can be denied.
But whether the interpersonal contacts so important to the conduct of Senate business have been seriously damaged is another
matter.

Friendship among U.S. senators is a habitually misunder-
stood feature of the upper chamber. Few senators are buddies,
although there was more social interaction outside the walls of
the Senate in the past than there is now. What senators call
friendship, and what is vitally important to the smooth operation of the Senate, is a kind of stable business relationship based
on trust and reciprocity that grows up between people who may
have never exchanged a confidence, or traded volleys on a
tennis court, or drunk bourbon together. Hostility among senators also tends to run in fairly narrow channels. Almost all
senators profess distaste for highly dogmatic and inflexible colleagues, and there are always a few senators in every era pointed
to by their fellow members as troublesome and obstructionist,
but widespread and enduring uncivility is not characteristic of
the Senate. Even a chaotic Senate is not necessarily a vicious
and unfriendly place.[13]

Among the fourteen senators and former senators with

House service who were interviewed, there was unanimous agreement that senators were overburdened, and that staff members handled much more office-to-office negotiation. All, however, felt that interpersonal comity was still a defining feature of the Senate and none felt that the House and Senate were at all alike in terms of the quality of member-on-member dealings.

Senators as different in temperament and philosophy as Montana Democrat Max Baucus and Texas Republican Phil Gramm emphasized the greater importance of the personal touch in the Senate than in the House and the greater disposition to tolerate deviant, even egregiously bad, behavior. They also observed that, unlike the House, you might conceivably have to deal with all ninety-nine of your colleagues. Baucus recalled: "I found that in the House I dealt with a good number of members personally but rarely with any others. Over here it is different. The variety and spectrum of who you deal with is proportionately much greater than in the House." Gramm observed, "I could give you three or four names right off the bat of people who are just genuinely disliked—who are notorious for being obnoxious and abusive—but people don't call their hand. The rules are such that it's better to tolerate it than get all stirred up."

Senators who served before 1980 make much the same observation. John Culver, who felt, on the whole, that the House and Senate were becoming more alike, qualified his endorsement of convergence by observing, "There's a lot more logrolling in the Senate. Also there's the feeling that if I get it through the Senate and write my press release, I'll drop it in conference because I've done my thing politically. So everybody in the Senate is just a lot more accommodating in terms of the political interests of the members than the House can afford to be." Culver's observation about the prevalence of Senate logrolling, or swapping political favors and voting for colleagues' bills on the expectation that the gesture will be returned, was shared by all those interviewed.

A number of the senators interviewed did, however, mention that they had detected a breakdown in Senate comity and a rise in interpersonal friction at the time the Republicans became the majority in the chamber in 1981. One senator who went out of his way to comment on this period was Michigan Democrat Donald Riegle.

When the Republicans won control of the Senate on the strength of Reagan's victory in 1980, they achieved in the Senate a remarkable degree of political and partisan solidarity and that introduced into the Senate a somewhat higher level of partisanship. I think, generally speaking, it was less than in the House but I think it was higher than it had been before 1981.

If Riegle's judgment is correct, an observer looking at the Senate in the early 1980s might well have come to the conclusion that comity had declined. Republicans in both chambers were remarkably cohesive in support of the Reagan administration's programs, but this hardening of partisan lines was a strange and unfamiliar sensation for many senators.

It was during this period that Kansas Republican Bob Dole took over the chairmanship of the Finance Committee from longtime chairman Russell Long (D-La.). Dole began to hold closed-door meetings for the Republican members of the committee. On one occasion Long attempted to gain entry to such a meeting and was turned away at the door by a staff member who informed the astonished former chairman that it was a Republicans-only meeting.

Long, who believed that revenge is always more tasty when eaten cold, bided his time. In short order, the Reagan administration proposed to withhold any taxes that might be due the federal government on interest or dividend payments at the time the payments were made to customers by banks or businesses rather than have the recipients pay when they filed their taxes. It was basically a scheme to get money to the Treasury more quickly. The plan came under attack by Wisconsin Republican Bob Kasten, who characterized it as an attack on people living on fixed incomes. Kasten, however, was a junior member who had arrayed against him both the White House and Finance Committee chairman Dole.

Then, with no apparent motive, Russell Long threw his considerable prestige into the battle on Kasten's side. Dole asked why he was opposing a plan that seemed to be such a good policy. Long is reported to have reminded Dole about the partisan meeting and the door that had been slammed in his face. With Long's assistance, Kasten's effort to block the administration plan succeeded and Dole had occasion in defeat to reflect upon the price that is paid in the Senate for excessive partisanship and disrespect to a senior colleague of whatever party.

The importance of good collegial relationships seems to be well understood even by the newest members of the Senate. If there has been a long-term decline in the importance of collegiality, it was not to be found in the views of Senator Timothy Wirth (D-Colo.), elected in 1986.

One of the things that's so impressive about this place is the personal relationships that exist over here. Because of the filibuster and the fact that so much gets done by unanimous consent and the comity that's needed to support that kind of system, what grows up is a great deal of personal rapport among members of the Senate that is real.

People talk about this place being a club. It has to be a club in order to get unanimous consent. But underneath that grow up very strong, very real relationships. It takes a while to develop those relationships so that people know your style and approach enough to trust you and take you seriously.

Again, it appears that a snapshot in time taken in the early 1980s showed a Senate that was uncharacteristically partisan due, in large measure, to the unfamiliarity of Republicans with the sensation of being the majority party in the chamber.

High turnover in the personnel of the Senate in some recent elections gave credence to the image of a more transitory and anomic membership. The elections of 1978 and 1980 were notable for the large number of new senators produced. The Senate that was sworn in on January 15, 1979, had twenty new members and there were eighteen freshman on hand for induction on January 3, 1981. Reading these figures, one could easily conclude that turnover was destroying continuity in the Senate and making it a more anonymous and less collegial body. But the elections of 1982 and 1984 produced only twelve freshmen between them. The abnormally large number of thirteen casualties inflicted on the members in the 1986 elections did not, however, signal a return to high rates of turnover. It was probably a reflection of the weakness of those Republican senators elected on Ronald Reagan's coattails in 1980 who did not enjoy that advantage six years later. By 1988, with the election of ten new senators the turnover rate came close to the post-1960 average of eleven Senate freshmen for each new Congress. Seen in this context, the 1978 and 1980 elections were abnormal but could well lead an observer in the early 1980s to conclude that turnover was changing the nature of the Senate.

Is it also the case that "recent House members rank with Senate celebrities in public recognition and/or acclaim"?[14] The rise or fall in the bicameral stardom quotient is perhaps the most slippery indicator of convergence or nonconvergence. While Speaker O'Neill, as the highest-ranking national Democrat in the years 1981–1987, was certainly a celebrity, his successor, Jim Wright, was a much less distinctive or public person, but then again, so was Senate Majority Leader Robert C. Byrd, who succeeded the telegenic Bob Dole. It is below the level of formal leadership that one looks for the prevalence of stardom in a legislative body, and recognizable faces constitute a much greater proportionate share—probably even in absolute numbers—of the Senate than the House.

It can be safely asserted that 10 percent of the Senate is recognizable to citizens of average political awareness by restricting the list to only those senators who have been recent presidential hopefuls or candidates and leaving out such familiar faces as Bradley, Helms, and Moynihan. Can any but the *cognoscenti* identify 10 percent (forty-four members) of the

House? Can any educated layperson, indeed, identify ten members of the House?

Another expression of convergence would be a decline in the loyalty on the part of its members to the Senate. And one measure of that institutional loyalty is whether or not senators want to remain there. Was the fact that three of the twelve presidential hopefuls of both parties as of January 1988 were incumbent senators an indication of flagging loyalty to the Senate? The three senators who did run hedged their bets and neither Dole, Gore, nor Simon quit the Senate to seek the White House. Texas law even allowed Senator Lloyd Bentsen to run simultaneously for vice-president and senator, thus leaving him a fall-back position in the event that the Dukakis ticket failed to win the 1988 presidential election. While three relatively young senators declined to seek new terms in 1988, you certainly saw no senators giving up their seats to run for governor or for the House. And while senators have always been among the most available presidential candidates, this is not evidence of a permanent decline in institutional loyalty in the Senate.

If we look to the words of senators themselves, there is often criticism of the Senate for its archaic and often anarchic ways, but little real Senate bashing. Indeed, the sense of satisfaction at being a senator or having been one is uniform across the fourteen people who served in both bodies.

I asked all the senators I interviewed whether they had ever had any second thoughts about leaving the House for the Senate. The responses varied only in the vehemence of their assertion of the superiority of the Senate.

From liberal Democrat Don Riegle came the statement: "I like the chance to make things happen in a direct way. I think that opportunity is available only in the Senate." Conservative Republican Phil Gramm simply said, "I'm glad to be out of the House." From eighty-six-year-old former senator Hugh Scott, who came to the House in 1941 and the Senate in 1959, there was this recollection: "I was totally elated to be in the Senate; completely exuberant about it. If I missed anything about the

House, it was the luncheons of the Pennsylvania delegation, but as for the proceedings of the House, it was a large disorganized team hitting pop flies into the infield." From forty-seven-year-old Max Baucus, who entered the House in 1974 and the Senate in 1978, came this appraisal of his decision to run for the Senate: "It's clear to me personally that I made the right decision. One has greater opportunity to develop issues that interest one and, historically, senators have been able to marshal constituencies outside their own state."

These were not uncritical judgments. Timothy Wirth faulted the Senate's technological backwardness. Max Baucus lamented the loss of the circle of friends he had in the House. Don Riegle, Chris Dodd, and Paul Sarbanes deplored the loss of intimacy that comes when you trade a congressional district for a state. Virtually everyone complained about obstruction-ism and delay in the legislative process but none expressed anything but the most qualified and attenuated nostalgia for the House and none proclaimed the Senate to be nothing more than a downsized House or wanted it to move in that direction.

One factor that appeared to be both a symptom and a cause of the decline in interpersonal comity detected in the early 1980s was the role of staff. In Chapter 3 I discussed the greater prominence of staff in the Senate than in the House but made only passing note of its effect on senators' relations with col-leagues. In David Kozak's study of sixteen senators, the promi-nence of staff was a commonly cited difference between House and Senate. One of Kozak's respondents complained, in the context of a discussion of staff, "You don't see the other sena-tors that much. We are more isolated from our colleagues."[15] Unquestionably, the modern Senate office does resemble a small corporation in both numbers and complexity. Much office-to-office contact is carried on by staff members. But it would be a mistake to conclude that the important bilateral and multilat-eral agreements among senators are cooked up by the staffs and merely rubber-stamped by the senators. Interoffice consulta-tions among staff typically take place only after the principals involved—the senators themselves—have authorized negotiations. Senate staff, for all its importance, rarely does anything more than implement decisions made by senators who have agreed on the broad outlines of a deal. As the staff member of the freshman Democrat quipped, it is, in the final analysis, *"mano a mano."*

Senator Timothy Wirth asserted, "More business gets done among members here than in the House. In the House you assign your staff people to work it out because there are so many members in the House. Over here, you don't get anything done unless you talk personally to the other guy."

What Wirth says does not detract from the relatively greater importance of the staff on the Senate side than on the House side but it does tell us that for all of the buffering and cosseting, senators have not become complete creatures of their staffs and that deals must still be struck among principals, not their agents. Senators are almost certainly more poorly informed on details than their House colleagues, and more apt to use staff expertise to fill gaps, but they are in no way inferior to House members in discerning the politics of a situation or even in simply being well informed enough about the substance of policy to make sound decisions with their colleagues.

COMING TO TERMS: IS THE SENATORIAL MARGIN OF COMFORT VANISHING?

There is considerable support for at least part of the third element of convergence theory and that is that the difference between the two-year term of House members and the six-year term of senators has narrowed because of a high attrition rate at the polls for incumbent senators. Apprehensive about defeat, many senators have expanded the active phase of their campaigning to the point where they resemble House members.

Traditionally, the difference between the abbreviated House term and the elongated Senate term was so great that the Senate was looked upon as a kind of semi-retirement. House Speaker Thomas Brackett Reed (1889–1891 and 1895–1899) thought so little of the activity level of the upper chamber that he described the Senate as a place where good representatives go when they die. During the time when election to the Senate was by vote of the state legislature, the combination of insulation from popular control and length of term made the Senate a very safe and relaxed place to be. James A. Garfield, who served in the House for seventeen years, believed that the necessity to stand for election every two years was injurious to health and that, at the very least, "a seat in the Senate will delay the catastrophe."[16]

Representative Oscar W. Underwood, an Alabama Democrat, who was serving as majority leader of the House in the aftermath of the great Democratic triumph in 1912, found life in a House leadership position so taxing that "his wife felt he might find sanctuary in the Senate."[17] At the same time, however, "Senator John Bankhead, the senior senator, and other friends counseled him against surrendering his tenacious hold on the Ninth District Congressional seat for the uncertainties of a Senate campaign."[18]

These "uncertainties" were part of a new set of considerations that attended the ratification of the Seventeenth Amendment in 1913. With the disappearance of the margin of safety provided by the state legislatures, the principal buffer left to senators was the six-year term. The political calculation for would-be senators became more complicated. Those who occupied safe House seats, like Underwood, would have to strike a balance between the more perilous new electoral environment of the U.S. senator and the potential for more influence. George W. Norris, a Nebraska Republican and prominent progressive, had his eyes on the future when he pondered a run for the Senate in 1912, the last congressional election before the ratification of the direct-election amendment, and "decided to risk the chances of promotion to the Senate. There, crowded chambers and stifling procedure could not silence an outspoken man."[19]

With the removal of the political insulation of state legislative elections that often produced senators who were under the thumb of political bosses but whose safety was assured, the six-year term loomed more impressively as a safety margin. Sometimes, the allure of the six-year term in the Senate, with its promise of vastly greater influence, had a practical appeal as well. Consider the calculations made by Democratic House member Estes Kefauver of Tennessee when he considered a run in 1948 against incumbent senator Arthur T. "Tom" Stewart.

Against his loss of House seniority and his assurance of effective support in his home district, the Senate would offer a stronger power base from which to work toward realization of his legislative objectives. . . . There were strong personal considerations, too: he did not want his children to be reared in an apartment, but he was reluctant to buy a house when he had to face the risk of being retired from Congress every two years.[20]

Despite the fact that "Kefauver was established solidly as a representative and could be elected as long as he wished to stay in the House," he defended to his father his decision to run for the Senate with the argument that " 'I've served long enough in the House . . . I can't keep on living in an apartment and running for reelection every two years. My family deserves a normal life, in a home of their own.' "[21] Kefauver defeated Stewart in 1948 and went on to spend the next fifteen years in the Senate.

What is so remarkable about the apparent safety of House seats is that the obligation to run every two years—even if it amounts to no more than a formality—generates apprehension in many House members. "House members see electoral uncertainty where outsiders would fail to unearth a single objective indicator of it."[22] House members fear general elections, and if general elections are no problem because of the partisan cast of the district, they obsess about primaries. If they fear that they will be overtaken by complacency, they fret about redistricting. The impressive margins by which so many House members win reelection and the consistent success of their reelection bids seem to be little compensation for the fact that every two-year interval could turn out to be a hinge of history, a climactic event.

House members are aware that the attachments of voters are not to the political party with which the candidates identify but to more flimsy and transient factors of a more personal nature. Members who find favor with the voters in one election can find themselves out of favor two years later. Without strong party attachments on the part of the voters to draw upon, House members must rise or fall on their own merits or short-comings.[23]

House members, when transported to the Senate, tend to see the electoral vulnerabilities differently. In the discussion of con-gressional districts and states in Chapter 4, there was a feeling on the part of most senators interviewed that a kind of intimacy prevailed in the relationship between a House member and his district that had few parallels in the bonds between senators and their states. Only among those senators from states with only two congressional districts and the one who had served at large was this sense of lost intimacy not pronounced. But what might look very comfortable from the Senate does not, evidently, put many minds to rest in the House. In the Senate, with its vastly more complicated and politically perilous terrain, the House district does seem almost pastoral in its simplicity and coziness, but for those still in the House, fate is never tempted with complacency.

Despite House members' own apprehensions about reelec-tion, senators who once served in the House regard the obliga-tion of their former colleagues to go before the voters every two years as something of a formality. Senator Paul Sarbanes, a Maryland Democrat said, "Look. People talk about congress-men having to run every two years. Well, if they have a mar-ginal district, that's a real problem. But most of them don't have marginal districts. Most of them have safe districts and they are not, in any real sense, running every two years."

Senator James Abourezk stressed the protection afforded by the six-year term but added an important qualification:

After a while in the Senate you say, "Jesus, God, they're running all the time over there in the House and I don't have to run. It's my second year and I'm still in office and they're opening doors for me and cheering my speeches and laughing at my jokes. My God, I might just forget to go home." Well, House members never forget to go back home. They're forced to and Senate members that don't are the ones that lose.

Evidence of the diminution of the importance of the term differential between House and Senate is found in the fund-raising behavior of senators. The trend toward earlier and almost-continual fund-raising activity was detected in the early 1980s.[24] Unlike senators of the past, who waited until their reelection year to raise funds in earnest, modern senators are spending their fifth or even fourth years in intensive fund-raising activities, and their first in paying off the previous campaign.

The reason for this preemptive fund-raising among senators is that their opponents are more likely than House challengers to attract media attention. Only a media-based strategy by an incumbent can ward them off. Incumbents can get a great deal of free media, but they are also forced to buy it at rates that have climbed into the stratosphere.

A six-year term in the United States Senate lasts 2,189 days. The cost of the average Senate campaign is now about $3 million. Setting aside a few days for vacation, this means that the average senator must raise $1,600 a day for every day in office. This breaks down to $100 for every waking hour.[25] It has also become something of an axiom in political campaigning that "early" money is better than "late" money. A sizable war chest of an incumbent can have the effect of deterring a challenger. Raising money, accordingly, becomes not only a resource for waging a campaign against a challenger but a strong disincentive for a potential rival to even think of becoming a declared challenger.

For twelve of the fourteen senators interviewed, the principal expression of convergence is in this trend toward almost-continual campaigning. The most pointed expression of this trend is in the expansion of fund-raising activities to encompass practically the entire six-year term. All of the senators who addressed this element of convergence condemned the trend very strongly.

Many lobbyists seem equally distressed. David Rubinstein, a former high official in the Carter White House who was later associated with a major Washington law firm, said, "Senators always have had their hand out. They're raising money for elections that have limitless costs. California, New York—you can never raise enough money and because of that feeling of never having enough money, you're always raising it."

The tone of dismay was captured by former senator John Culver of Iowa: "Nowadays senators come in with debts and the financial stresses of the campaign. They owe people money and the only way to get it is to go to the special interests right away rather than have that grace period of four or five years that was intended for them to be able to take a second look at the House judgment on the public policy question and give it a sober, reflective look."

Without question, the Senate as an institution now resonates to changes in the mood of the electorate in a manner dramatically at variance with the plan of the framers of the Constitution while the House seems immune to them. The high turnover in the Senate and the remarkable stability of the House seem to be producing a "devolution of the lower house into a relatively inflexible repository of stable, local interests and the associated birth of a popular upper house, functioning as a sensitive barometer of national mood."[26] What is less clear is whether this is causing changes in the behavior of senators away from the "sober and reflective" role described by Culver.

If it is true that the traditional respite from campaign activities on the part of U.S. senators has given way to a term-long period of fund-raising, have senators generally trimmed their sails to the prevailing political winds? Has the period of senatorial statesmanship, in which a measure of political boldness might be practiced, given way to greater caution and a tendency to behave according to the perceived wishes of the constituency?

One very obvious indication that senators are becoming more like House members in their relations with their constituencies is the growing frequency of trips from Washington back to the state. The percentage of House members who go home about once a week was as recently as 1980 far greater than the percentage of senators who do. The percentage of senators who visited their state less frequently than every two weeks was much higher than that of House members.[27]

Senators traditionally were not as diligent in fence-mending as a group as House members, but after the debacles of 1980 and 1986 at least some senators are emulating the attentiveness of congressmen. Senator Alfonse D'Amato (R-N.Y.) proudly calls himself a "pothole senator" as a badge of honor for his attentiveness to his constituency. When D'Amato's colleague from New York, Democratic Senator Daniel Patrick Moynihan (characterized by one journalist as a "scholar-senator"), visited the upstate city of Elmira, the local paper noted that "it took Moynihan six years to return." Elsewhere in the paper, it was reported that D'Amato had visited the town ten times.[28]

Senators are now using communications techniques such as "postal-patron" mailings that blanket the state and organizing town meetings to meet voters face-to-face. While these House-tested techniques for political success are finding much more favor among senators, and while some might even relish the designation "pothole senator," others, for a variety of reasons, will not emulate the conduct of House members.

Different styles have always prevailed in the Senate, ranging from those who think of themselves as instructed delegates who, as one senator put it, "are as nervous as a Christmas goose" on every vote for fear that it will be out of line with the wishes of the state to those who are almost defiantly independent. As Donald R. Matthews wrote in 1960, "a constituency as large as a state can be 'represented' in many different ways."[29]

The fact that the period of active fund-raising on the part of senators has expanded or that senators now resort to "postal-patron" mass mailings or even that they go home more often does not necessarily mean that they are more timid or compliant or that they are trying to ape House members. Research on legislators at both the state and national levels shows that they make major adjustments as election time nears. They may bring their voting behavior more in line with their legislative colleagues or they may establish a pattern of voting that is closer to the ideological middle.[30] They may also alter their pre-election voting habits to adjust to the characteristics of their likely challengers.[31]

What does it mean when senators become cautious as reelection time nears? The most straightforward explanation is that they hope such modifications will enable them to win reelection. But it also means that they think that their preexisting behavior has not been entirely compliant with the wishes of the voters. To bring your votes or statements more in line with constituent views or likely opponents or to camouflage yourself by voting like the average of your colleagues suggests that senators believe themselves to have been too independent or to have shown maverick or even radical tendencies. Put more bluntly, "many senators spend the majority of their time consciously and deliberately behaving in a manner they realize will not please their constituents to the maximum extent possible."[32]

Senators also show no increased inclination to take on only uncontroversial issues or those that have a direct connection with the interests of their states. Senators continue to pursue issues that are of personal concern to them. This has led one researcher to conclude, "The common cynical view of senators that their legislative efforts reflect a mindless pursuit of electoral goals is not close to the mark." Indeed, he adds, "Most senators value their unique position in the political system and most use it to pursue issues that they consider important."[33]

It is, of course, not necessarily the case that all state issues are politically safe for senators and all national issues are politically risky. Most senators raise funds nationally, so their willingness to tackle less parochial issues may simply be a reflection of their new dependence on campaign money from outside their state rather than evidence of statesmanship. Nonetheless, "senators are inundated with requests [to take up causes]. . . . In contrast, many House members go begging for attention, are constantly on the prowl for some way to get more involved, and are envious of the ability of senators to steal their claim to the leading role on surfacing national issues."[34]

THE PERSISTENCE OF PATTERNS OF
SPECIALIZATION AND GENERALITY

The fourth major area in which House-Senate convergence was detected in the early 1980s was in the degree of specialization and generalization that had hitherto been such a definitive difference between the two bodies. It was accepted wisdom that "it is the grand design of national public policy rather than the nitty-gritty details of legislation that is of prime concern to most senators."[35] The revisionist view was expressed by Norman Ornstein: "Committee and subcommittee assignments have proliferated, spreading House members much thinner. . . . The Senate has moved away from its focus on debate and deliberation towards a preoccupation with legislative nitty-gritty."[36]

The argument that the roles of the House and Senate on specialization have not merely converged but actually reversed receives little support from the fourteen senators interviewed. While the group does consist of both incumbents and former senators, the views of the ex-senators are valuable because all are still actively involved in lobbying and legal work associated with Congress. There was no difference, moreover, in the views of serving senators and former senators.

Texas Republican Phil Gramm asserted, "Senators are still by and large generalists. They are just involved in a lot more issues than House members. . . . They are people who are spread

thin and on a short cord." Michigan Democrat Don Riegle
made the case that there are simply practical limits to the
amount of specializing a senator can do.

You have just so much waterfront to cover around here that the best
you can hope for is to be knowledgeable on the subject matter of your
committee.

You're expected to be an advocate for your entire state and the
press expects you to be conversant on foreign policy matters. You're
expected to be a knowledgeable person. I think that House members
are just not under the same burden to the same degree; they really can
concentrate on just a few things.

Pennsylvania Republican Richard Schweiker saw the senator's opportunities to diversify as a salient difference between
the two chambers and also pointed to the difference in committee structures as the source of the difference: "There's more of
an opportunity to work in the field of your choice in the Senate:
to pick and choose. You really aren't in that kind of straitjacket
they have in the House where the only chance you have to get
a shot at something is through your committee. With only a
hundred senators available for so many committees, there's no
way in the world you're going to get the kind of specialization
they have in the House."

Recently, Steven S. Smith has argued that even with the
greater variety of committee assignments available to senators,
they are developing areas of concentration and leadership on
issues that do not fit in neatly with the jurisdictions of the
committees on which they serve.[37]

All the senators agreed that if they were to seize all the
opportunities that come by, they would be overwhelmed. Even
by picking and choosing many senators feel that they are being
pulled in a hundred different directions. All agreed with Maryland Democrat Paul Sarbanes's verdict that "the job, to some
degree, overwhelms you, whereas in the House you get much
more of a sense of being in control of your job." There was,
however, also a consensus around another Sarbanes observa-

tion: "The Senate gives you a scope you just don't have in the House."

It is undeniably the case that many House members are taking a much more expansive view of their roles than was the case traditionally. And it is also beyond dispute that there are senators who relish specialization. But there are simple, practical limits to the degree to which senators can specialize.

There is, moreover, in the Senate, a kind of inexorable force that can elevate the sights of even the most locally minded "pothole senator." Indeed, it has happened in the case of the very man who coined the phrase, New York Republican Alfonse D'Amato.

D'Amato's first public manifestation of concern about the drug policy in New York City was to don a battered army field jacket and visit the East Village of Manhattan as part of a media event to publicize his concern. But the broader implications of the drug problem were not lost on the senator, and he became one of the harshest and most vocal critics of Panama's dictator General Manuel Noriega and of U.S. drug policy in general. In a like manner, his parochial concern about the effects of acid rain on the lakes in the Adirondack Mountains of New York State led to an interest in national environmental policy that often put him at odds with the Reagan administration. While D'Amato still prides himself on his local focus, the implications of those parochial problems are being drawn in broader strokes.[38]

REVERTING TO TYPE ON THE ROLE OF LEADERSHIP

Finally, there is the question of the dispersion of power in the House so that "hierarchical positions, whether in the formal party leadership or at the top of committees, mean much less today than they did in the 1960s; 'leadership on specific issues can come from any of 400 or more sources . . .' More and more, the House is an ad hoc institution, without firm control over its own schedule or priorities—much like the Senate."[39]

Here again, a snapshot of bicameralism taken in the early

1980s may well have produced an image that has faded over time. It is unquestionably true that the great dispersion of formal power that took place in the House in the 1970s continues to give representatives many forums for the raising of issues—forums that were once very few in number. The great power enjoyed by twenty chairmen of standing committees that caused them to be called, only half-jokingly, the "College of Cardinals" has diminished. Moreover, in the early 1980s, with the Democrats holding only the most tenuous control of the House because of the practice of conservative "Boll Weevil" Democrats to vote with a highly cohesive Republican minority, the control of the Speaker was indeed problematical.

A contemporary view of the House, however, yields a picture much more in line with the classical view of this chamber as a place where real influence reposes in very few hands. As journalist Alan Ehrenhalt puts it, "The current House is democratic in the sense that all members, even the most junior ones, are part of the debate. But when it comes to making decisions, democracy is the wrong word to use."[40]

Representative Phil Sharp (D-Ind.), who has served in the House for more than a dozen years, observed, "The natural tendency of this institution is toward oligarchy. . . . What we have now is a technique for returning to a closed system where a few people make all the decisions."[41] The reassertion of the oligarchical nature of the House comes from two sources: the basic structural reality that a large and cumbersome body like the House simply cannot function with too many power sources, and the more short-run factor of the "four-bill" Congress where all may debate but few have any real impact on important legislation. So while membership in the traditional oligarchy came with the chairmanship of a standing committee, the new "College of Cardinals" consists of those chairs whose committees either enjoy unusually broad jurisdiction (Energy and Commerce) or process "must-pass" legislation (Appropriations and its thirteen subcommittees, Ways and Means, and Budget). Other House committees such as Foreign Affairs may serve as excellent pulpits for individual members, but a high level of activity on the part of a few members should not be confused with influence.

There is no doubt that opportunities do exist for entrepreneurial House members and that, on occasion, individuals who are not assigned to the most active committees can have an important impact. The case of Representative Charles Schumer (D-N.Y.) and the role he played in passage of the 1986 immigration reform bill is one that is cited to support the assertion that there are opportunities for influence on the part of rank-and-file members who do not serve on prestige committees. This led Burdett Loomis to argue that "the oligarchy of the 1980s is a permeable one, subject to penetration by skilled, activist members."[42]

To acknowledge that House members are more free to pursue issues and causes and that some of them are successful tells us that the House has changed, but we cannot make a clear-cut case for convergence because it does not tell us that most House members now look like most senators.

The Persistence of House-Senate Differences

While the House and Senate have changed individually in many important respects and are different places than they were fifty years ago, they have not converged to the point where an observer could say that the differences between them are now trivial. Important distinctions persist and they are distinctions that define dramatically the differences between the two houses.

The average senator enjoys a degree of personal influence that the average House member cannot even dream of. While one could point to examples of influential House members and powerless senators, that is not the norm. Indeed, a rank-and-file senator who had less of an impact on policy than a House back-bencher would be considered by most experts on Congress to be incompetent.

The importance of interpersonal relations and comity among colleagues is every bit as important in the Senate as it ever was. It could be seen in the obsessive concern with bipartisanship in the debate to confirm former senator John Tower as secretary of defense in 1989. In any organization in which so much business is expedited through the use of unanimous consent, agreements cannot trample cavalierly on collegial sensitivities. The House is not immune from such imperatives but the sensibilities of its least member are not a preoccupation of a leadership that is concerned with raw numbers, not concurrent majorities. The House can ignore the tantrums of the deviant or disaffected and may elevate to leadership posts disputatious figures such as Republican Whip Newt Gingrich, chosen by his colleagues in 1989 for his fierce partisanship.

While leadership in the House is variable in its authoritativeness, it is almost always more despotic than Senate leadership. Senate leaders, however, are certainly not without instruments of chastisement. Many a senator during Robert C. Byrd's long reign as majority leader learned that, however limited the cudgels of party leadership, Byrd's position on the Appropriations Committee enabled him to reward and punish colleagues with some consistency. But not every Senate leader has the leverage of an important committee at his disposal, and even Byrd is still known to call a colleague "Boss." Such a gesture by a House leader to a junior colleague would probably be thought of as condescending.

Senators appear, however, to have learned two important lessons from House members: the necessity to perform those dreary but necessary chores associated with constituent casework, and the need to raise money early and often. Senators have in recent years become somewhat more attentive to visits to the constituency although they apparently have not reached the heights of diligence found in the House. Town meetings have also become more common senatorial activities. It may well be that the 95 percent reelection success rate of House members in recent years has become so dazzling to the more vulnerable senators that they have followed the members' lead. In most states, however, there are practical limits to such a strategy.

A novel explanation of the more constituency-oriented senator is offered by Senator Chris Dodd of Connecticut, who lays the new emphasis to a generational change. Dodd points out that while many senators come from the House, where such ombudsmanship and social work are common, newer senators have had experience with the Peace Corps, VISTA, and other voluntary agencies and many came to political maturity during the 1960s when notions of participatory democracy were at their fullest flowering. The new service orientation, then, is not so much an act of emulation or even transference from the more casework-intensive House, but rather a more complex phenomenon with its roots in the personal characteristics of younger senators.

Despite much complaining about everything from workload to the absence of up-to-date computer systems, no senator I interviewed expressed opinions that could, by any stretch of the imagination, be considered scornful of the Senate. In only one interview with an incumbent senator did I detect feelings of loss as the result of leaving the House, and that individual deplored only the diminished sense of intimacy with his smaller House constituency. Yet it is clear that at least some former House members fail to make the adjustment and look upon their period of service in the House as their Homeric age. George McGovern spoke of a few who, he thought, had suffered from the transition:

The late Lee Metcalf (D-Mont.) was never happy in the Senate. I think it was because he was totally overshadowed by his senior colleague, Mike Mansfield. In the House he had been a kind of leader of the young Turks consisting of maybe a hundred people.

The same thing is true of Gene McCarthy (D-Minn.). I don't know McCarthy well but my impression was that he loved his days in the House and never really enjoyed the Senate where he was overshadowed by Hubert Humphrey.

In the House we would talk about McCarthy's Marauders. He along with Metcalf had great influence with the younger and more liberal members of the House but I always felt that both McCarthy

202 HOUSE AND SENATE

and Metcalf lapsed into a sort of cynical, almost apathetic, role in the Senate. They just didn't like the slow pace and the deferential business that went on over there.

Richard Fenno has focused some of his research on the dynamics of senatorial adjustment and it is clear that some people have difficulty making the adjustment to the Senate and others probably never make it at all, even those with prior experience in the House. With hopes so high for the more relaxed, influential, and visible senatorial career, it is not surprising that some find it less glamorous than they had anticipated and become disillusioned.

Predictability has probably declined somewhat in both houses but the consensus of those interviewed is that the Senate is more apt to spring surprises for no other reason than the almost unlimited discretion that senators have in introducing nongermane amendments—acts obviated by House rules and the Argus-eyed vigilance of the Rules Committee. Scheduling seems more problematic in both places and there was much criticism of leaders who impose deadlines that usually cannot be met.

THE PERSISTENCE OF THE PRESTIGE DIFFERENTIAL

One indication of a coalescence of the House and Senate and a blurring of the lines of institutional distinction might be found in evidence that the Senate had slipped in general prestige and the House had gained. While none of those who made the case for convergence suggested that the prestige differential that had always favored the modern Senate had narrowed, evidence of a diminution of the prestige gap would be an important indicator of convergence. If, for example, there was evidence that the Senate was ceasing to act as a magnet for House members seeking political advancement, one might comfortably infer convergence. That is assuredly not the case. Of the class of senators elected in November 1986, nine of thirteen either had come directly from the House or had prior House service. Since

1789, almost 600 House members have made the trek from the south side of the Capitol to the north; a mere handful of senators or former senators has made the trip south. In the 101st Congress, only former senator Claude D. Pepper (D-Fla.) served in the House after having previously served in the Senate. Thirty-eight senators had served previously in the House.

Another sign of institutional convergence might be seen in the equalization in the number of presidential aspirants coming out of each chamber. Historically, senators have always been among the most eligible group of officeholders lining up for presidential nominations. Since the Civil War, senators have constituted the largest group of contenders at national presidential nominating conventions. Over the period from 1868 to 1972, with 31 of 102 contenders, they outnumber all other groups of major officeholders such as governors, vice-presidents, members of the House, and federal appointees such as Cabinet members. The only other category of officeholders that comes close is governors with 29 contenders. In one period only—from 1892 until 1916—were House members more numerous than senators in the ranks of hopefuls at convention time. Between 1868 and 1972, however, House members constituted less than 10 percent of contenders, with only 10 of 102 hopefuls coming from the House.[43]

In the period from 1976 to the present, only four incumbent or recent House members were considered as serious presidential hopefuls: Arizona Democrat Morris Udall in 1976; Illinois Republican John Anderson in 1980; and Representatives Richard Gephardt and Jack Kemp in 1988. During this same period fifteen senators (seventeen, if former vice-presidents Humphrey and Mondale, who also served in the Senate, are counted) were contenders at some period in the course of the primary seasons. So the Senate continues to be the main source of presidential aspirants for both parties and the House only an occasional contributor. If serving as the nursery of presidents adds luster to an institution, the Senate is still more brightly burnished than the House.

But the recent successes of Governors Carter, Reagan, and Dukakis in securing nomination and, in two cases, election suggest that for all of their prominence as contenders, incumbent senators are not very good at winning nominations and are even less successful at gaining the presidency. Indeed, the last sitting senator to capture the White House was John F. Kennedy in 1960, and the only other twentieth-century incumbent senator was Warren G. Harding in 1920. As far as the national tickets of both parties are concerned, senators seem to be most useful as vice-presidential running mates who are chosen to act as insurance policies for good relations with Congress. Both Dan Quayle and Lloyd Bentsen were picked in 1988 with at least some weight given to their impact on congressional relations for a victorious presidential candidate.

More elusive but certainly influential as a factor differentiating the House and Senate is what Richard Fenno calls the "A Team–B Team" effect, whereby House members demonstrate symptoms of a kind of inferiority complex because they are forced into the shadow of senators and know that no senator ever aspires to a seat in the House.

The legislative career hierarchy was embellished upon by a man uniquely qualified to comment on House-Senate differences in prestige—former Indiana congressman Floyd Fithian, who made an unsuccessful try for the Senate and ended up serving as administrative assistant to Illinois senator Paul Simon. Fithian is the only former House member to serve as a staff member in the Senate.

My theory on American politics is that a person goes out and works their tail off to get elected to the state assembly for a two-year term and then an opportunity comes up because a state senator decides not to run again and they move up to that four-year state senate term as a normal path of progression. They have, quote unquote, advanced themselves.

Then, let's say the state senator gets elected to the U.S. House of Representatives, he has advanced himself. Now the next step higher on the rungs is the U.S. Senate. And you want to run for president. That is the progression.

There are, of course, some people in the House who have made a career of it—they've become Speaker or chairman or whatever. And these fellows wouldn't take a Senate seat if it were handed to them without competition. But those fellows are very, very few in number and the political graveyard is populated by all kinds of House members who wanted to become senators. And I'm one of them.

The status discrepancy between the two chambers can also be found in the different treatment accorded House members and senators by the executive branch of government. George Smathers, who represented Florida in the House from 1947 to 1951 and in the Senate from 1951 until 1969, described the difference this way:

You'd be someone who was thirty-four years in the House and call somebody downtown and they would say, "What was your name, again?" And you'd say, "I'm sorry, I'm Congressman So-and-so." And then they'd say, "Oh, yeah," and maybe you'd get some attention, but you didn't get much. But when you were a senator, it was a whole different ball game.

Smathers then recalled the treatment House members typically got from the White House.

I had been a member of the House for three and a half years before I ever got to go to the White House. And I got there only because Truman sent for me to try [unsuccessfully] to persuade me not to run against Claude Pepper. The only reason Truman knew me was because he used to vacation in Key West, which was in my congressional district, and he'd sometimes invite me to ride down with him. But that didn't happen to some congressmen from north Georgia. That kind of guy never got to see the president.

An indication that little has changed comes from Timothy Wirth (D-Colo.), elected to the Senate in 1986 after twelve years in the House: "A congressional liaison guy from the White House came by in 1981 right after Reagan's inauguration and introduced himself. Last week I got a call from the White House congressional liaison office asking me if I would help them on the INF Treaty. After I hung up the phone I realized that I had not talked to one of those guys at any time during the last seven years of my time in the House."

Differences so deeply rooted in the Constitution, in 200 years of custom and practice, and, above all, in the simple but stark difference in the size of the House and Senate, impose strict limits on the degree of convergence that could occur. There have been times that one chamber has taken on certain of the appearances of the other. There may even be a modest degree of emulation, but it usually does not generalize much beyond a very limited zone of imitation.

Most surprising, even for someone who has worked in both chambers, is the degree of isolation of the two bodies from each other. While one might hesitate to use the term "congressional apartheid," it would not be too wide of the mark. House and Senate occupy the same tiny island but the border between the two is well delineated. Border raids are repelled promptly and vigorously, as Senator Edward Kennedy learned when he attempted to get his nephew, Representative Joseph P. Kennedy II, a seat on the House Appropriations Committee. Cooperation beyond that which is dictated by the Constitution or by the specialized interests of members is limited. Partisan solidarity is a tiny hole in a fence and those periods of consistent bicameral cooperation between the institutional and party leaders of the House and Senate tend to develop at random. The most recent example of this was the period in the 1950s when Texas senator Lyndon B. Johnson and House Speaker Sam Rayburn, also a Texan and Democrat, worked closely together. Institutional differences always worked against this kind of cooperation, but party loyalty could mitigate the rigors of isolation. That bridge is now less sturdy, and when personal coolness prevails between the leaders of the two houses, the estrangement becomes more intense.

Even when both houses are under the control of the same

party and have leaders pledged to cooperation, the essential differences between the chambers can precipitate harsh feelings. Indeed, one of the first issues to be tackled by the 100th Congress in which both houses were under Democratic control for the first time in six years proved to be one that inflamed feelings on both sides of the Capitol. It was a pay raise for Congress. While senators and House members earn the same salary, senators have a history of less enthusiasm for pay raises than do House members because senators are, on average, wealthier than House members and can usually earn more than House members as outside speakers because of their greater visibility. Other bicameral spats followed the pay-raise imbroglio. There was a late-1987 impasse on an omnibus spending bill that House members blamed on the leisurely procedures of the Senate. Failure to come to timely agreement on aid to Nicaraguan rebels was likewise laid by House members to dilatory tactics by senators. With great bitterness, Representative Mike Synar (D-Okla.) complained, "The Senate is a mess. It's worse than it's ever been. House members are being held accountable for a Congress that's broken that they did not break."[44]

For those senators who have never served in the House, feelings toward the House are not even tempered with nostalgia. A former staff assistant to the late Frank Church of Idaho, who served as chairman of the Senate Foreign Relations Committee, said that his boss's feelings about the House amounted to a kind of phobia: "When Frank Church would drive home at night, he would never go down Independence Avenue. He'd go home down Constitution Avenue even though it was out of his way. He did that because the House buildings were on Independence Avenue and he would never go by the House buildings."

While interviewing a former member of the House, now a Washington lobbyist, I mentioned the observation by now-Senator Donald Riegle that the longer a member serves in the U.S. House of Representatives the more he comes to detest the Senate.

The former House member turned his swivel chair and gazed out of his window, seeming to be engrossed in thought. Slowly, a malicious smile began to spread across his face. "No," he said. "That certainly wasn't true in my case." Then he added, "I hated the Senate from the very first day I was in the House."

Senators, for their part, tend to be oblivious as to what the House members think of them. They do not deign to be angry. As Pennsylvania Republican Richard Schweiker recalled the relations between the two chambers, "There are these collective feelings but they run stronger one way than the other. The feeling in the House against the Senate is much stronger than the other way. If there was one term you had to keep using in the House it was 'the other body' when you talked about the Senate. Well, when you're a senator, you could care less whether you're called 'the other body' or not. You usually call the other place 'the House.' Now, you wouldn't rub it in and call it 'the lower house.' Senators don't believe in doing that."

I have attempted to build a case, thus far, that both the adversary and unitary forms of democracy are found in both houses of Congress but that the dominant expression in the House is adversary and the dominant manifestation in the Senate is unitary. David J. Vogler and Sidney R. Waldman, who applied Jane Mansbridge's framework of the two forms of democracy to Congress, stress the essential role of both forms. They state: "A policy decision, whether it is an adversary bargain struck among conflicting interests or a unitary agreement based on common interests, represents an end point of both types of democracy."[45]

But policy outcomes are only part of the picture, because "the democratic legitimacy of Congress rests on both the legislative process and the resulting policies."[46] This process meets its severest test when Congress is called upon to write legislation under the goad of public alarm and indignation. It was under such pressure that Congress was forced to fashion a policy to deal with the drug epidemic in American society. It was legislation that needed to meet the test of responsiveness to the needs of beleaguered and fearful constituents. But it also needed to meet the standard of legislation that was effective and consistent with a constitutional system that embraced all Americans. The final chapter tells how the two houses of Congress met that challenge working in characteristic ways.

NOTES

1. Bernard Mayo, *Henry Clay* (Boston: Houghton Mifflin, 1937), p. 271.
2. Ibid.
3. Nelson W. Polsby, "Strengthening Congress in National Policy-Making," *Yale Review,* 59 (June 1970), p. 487.
4. Alan Ehrenhalt, "Media, Power Shifts Dominate O'Neill's House," *Congressional Quarterly Weekly Report,* 44, September 13, 1986, p. 2135.
5. Ibid.
6. This encapsulated form of convergence theory is based on four important statements of the argument which are more elaborate and complex and deserve a thorough reading by anyone interested in exploring the question in detail: The four sources are: Norman J. Ornstein, "The House and the Senate in a New Congress," in Thomas E. Mann and Norman J. Ornstein, eds., *The New Congress* (Washington, D.C.: American Enterprise Institute, 1981), pp. 363–371; David C. Kozak, "House-Senate Differences: A Test Among Interview Data (or 16 U.S. Senators with House Experience Talk About the Differences)," in David C. Kozak and John D. Macartney, eds., *Congress and Public Policy,* 2d ed. (Chicago: Dorsey Press, 1987), pp. 79–84; Timothy E. Cook, "The Electoral Connection in the 99th Congress," *PS,* 19 (Winter 1986), pp. 15–22; and John R. Alford and John R. Hibbing, "Inverted Bicameralism: Electoral Sensitivity in the United States Congress," paper delivered at the annual meeting of the American Political Science Association, Washington, D.C., September 3–6, 1988.
7. Ornstein in Mann and Ornstein, eds., op. cit., p. 367.
8. Ibid., p. 368.
9. Alan Ehrenhalt, op cit., p. 2137.
10. Ornstein in Mann and Ornstein, eds., op. cit., p. 367.
11. Quoted in Tim Hackler, "What's Wrong with the U.S. Senate?" *American Politics,* 2 (January 1987), p. 7.
12. Quoted in Jacqueline Calmes, " 'Trivialized' Filibuster Is Still a Potent Tool," *Congressional Quarterly Weekly Report,* 45 (September 5, 1987), p. 2115.
13. For a fuller treatment of interpersonal relations among senators see Ross K. Baker, *Friend and Foe in the U.S. Senate* (New York: The Free Press, 1980).
14. Ornstein in Mann and Ornstein, eds., op. cit., p. 368.
15. Kozak in Kozak and Macartney, eds., op. cit., p. 86.
16. Margaret Leech and Harry J. Brown, *The Garfield Orbit* (New York: Harper and Row, 1978), p. 198. Garfield won a Senate seat in January 1880 for a term beginning on March 4, 1881, but having won, in the interim, the presidency of the United

States, declined to take his seat in the Senate. Inaugurated as president on March 4, 1881, he was shot on July 2, 1881, and died of gunshot wounds on September 19, 1881.

17. Evans C. Johnson, *Underwood: A Political Biography* (Baton Rouge, La.: Louisiana State University Press, 1980), p. 227.

18. Ibid.

19. Richard L. Neuberger and Stephen B. Kahn, *Integrity: The Life of George W. Norris* (New York: Vanguard Press, 1937), p. 48.

20. Charles L. Fontenay, *Estes Kefauver* (Knoxville, Tenn.: University of Tennessee Press, 1980), pp. 130–131.

21. Ibid., pp. 132–133.

22. Richard F. Fenno, Jr., *Homestyle* (Boston: Little, Brown, 1978), pp. 10–11.

23. Thomas E. Mann, *Unsafe at Any Margin* (Washington, D.C.: American Enterprise Institute, 1978), *passim.*

24. Richard F. Fenno, Jr., *The United States Senate: A Bicameral Perspective* (Washington, D.C.: The American Enterprise Institute, 1982), pp. 29–38.

25. "The Tin Cup Club," *The Washington Post National Weekly Edition,* July 6, 1987.

26. Alford and Hibbing, op. cit., p. 30.

27. Glenn R. Parker, "Sources of Change in Congressional District Attentiveness," *American Journal of Political Science* (February 1980), pp. 115–124.

28. Clifford D. May, "Moynihan Working on Image," *New York Times,* Monday, April 20, 1987.

29. Donald R. Matthews, *U.S. Senators and Their World* (New York: Random House, 1960) p. 237.

30. Richard C. Elling, "Ideological Change in the U.S. Senate: Time and Electoral Responsiveness," *Legislative Studies Quarterly,* 7 (February 1982), pp. 75–92.

31. Martin Thomas, "Election Proximity and Senatorial Roll Call Voting," *American Journal of Political Science,* 29 (February 1985), pp. 96–111.

32. Ibid., p. 111. See also Gerald C. Wright, Jr., and Michael B. Berkman, "Candidates and Policy in United States Senate Elections," *American Political Science Review,* 80 (June 1986), pp. 567–588, and Robert A. Bernstein and Michael B. Berkman, "Do Senators Moderate Strategically?" *American Political Science Review,* 82 (March 1988), pp. 237–245.

33. Steven S. Smith, "Informal Leadership in the Senate: Opportunities, Resources, and Motivations," paper prepared for the Project on Congressional Leadership of the Everett McKinley Dirksen Congressional Center and the Congressional Research Service, Washington, D.C., September 30, 1987, p. 10.

34. Ibid., p. 3.

35. Edward G. Carmines and Lawrence C. Dodd, "Bicameralism in Congress: The Changing Partnership," in Lawrence C. Dodd and Bruce I. Oppenheimer, eds., *Congressional Reconsidered,* 3d ed. (Washington, D.C.: CQ Press, 1985), p. 425.

36. Ornstein in Mann and Ornstein, eds., op. cit., pp. 368, 371.

37. Steven S. Smith, op. cit., pp. 5–6.

38. Clifford D. May, "Image of a Senator: D'Amato Sticks to Local Issues," *New York Times,* Wednesday, May 11, 1988.

39. Ornstein in Mann and Ornstein, eds., op. cit., p. 367.

40. Ehrenhalt, op. cit., p. 2136.

41. Ibid.

42. For a fuller treatment of the new House activists see Burdett Loomis, *The New American Politician* (New York: Basic Books, 1988).

43. Robert L. Peabody, Norman J. Ornstein, and David W. Rohde, "The United States

Senate as a Presidential Incubator: Many Are Called but Few Are Chosen," *Political Science Quarterly,* 91 (Summer 1976), pp. 237–258.

44. Janet Hook, "House-Senate Acrimony Bedevils Democrats," *Congressional Quarterly Weekly Report,* 46 (February 13, 1988), p. 296.

45. David J. Vogler and Sidney R. Waldman, *Congress and Democracy* (Washington, D.C.: Congressional Quarterly Press, 1985), p. 166.

46. Ibid.

7

The Persistence of Bicameral Distinctions and American Democracy

I T WAS THE ISSUE of the 1980s. It made the covers of news magazines and was often the lead story on the nightly newscasts. As journalistic reports multiplied, public indignation swelled. Demands were heard for a "czar" to be appointed to deal with the problem, with an office located just down the hall from the president's. It suffused popular culture from prime-time dramatic shows to public service spots. It was the favorite cause of prominent people from rap singers to the First Lady. The issue was drugs and how to stop the brazen, avaricious, violent purveyors of narcotics from polluting the nation with their wares. Reeling from nightly TV visuals of police using armored cars and battering rams and fighting off adversaries armed with rapid-fire weapons, Americans demanded an end to what came to be called the drug plague.

Members of Congress did not need to wait to be inundated by indignant mail to begin legislating to curtail the influx of drugs. Aware of the agenda-setting role of the media, they moved swiftly to draft tough—even draconian—measures to deter and punish drug smugglers and pushers. And with each new atrocity, the public demanded that the ante be raised against the drug criminals.

Characteristically, it was the House of Representatives that responded most promptly with a bill. By the time the members returned from their July 4th recess in 1986, legislation was ready to go to spur the nation's drive against illegal drugs.

The manner in which this bill and successor measures in 1988 developed and were modified in the House and Senate tells us much about contemporary bicameralism and recalls for us the original genius that gave it life and the current realities that give it vitality and relevance 200 years later.

That the effort to strike back dramatically at drug traffickers began in the House should come as no surprise to us. "Of all American political institutions, none is more sensitive to shifts in public sentiment than the House of Representatives. The House was designed that way by the Founding Fathers, who also created the Senate as a check on the passions that periodically sweep through that chamber."[1]

By some accounts it was the death on June 19, 1986, of University of Maryland's basketball star Len Bias from the use of cocaine that provided the dramatic impetus that spurred the House into action. Both Democrats and Republicans vied for the prize of being first with a drug bill, but a call from Speaker Tip O'Neill for a bipartisan approach to the problem was quickly followed by a pledge from Minority Leader Bob Michel that both the Democratic majority and the Republican minority would share in the authorship of the bill and, accordingly, the political credit. The two leaders struck a bargain: The legislation itself would be drafted by the Democrats, who controlled the committees, but the Republicans would be allowed to offer amendments on the floor of the House—and such a provision would be included in the rule granted by the Rules Committee, which is largely under the Speaker's control.[2]

The amendments to the House bill that passed the chamber on September 11, 1986, were drastic and punitive. They called for the federal death penalty in drug-related murders, the use of the armed forces of the United States to halt the flow of drugs into the country, and the relaxation of the so-called exclusionary rule which limits the kinds of procedures law enforcement officials can use to obtain evidence in criminal cases.

Within the Senate, amendments had surfaced that were similar to the ones in the House anti-drug bill. A group of Senate Democrats had proposed the creation of a "drug czar" with Cabinet status to coordinate the war on drugs. A group of Senate Republicans had introduced legislation imposing the death penalty, relaxing the exclusionary rule, and involving the armed forces.

Mirroring the spirit of bipartisanship already set in the House, Senate Democratic leader Robert C. Byrd (then in the minority) and Republican leader Bob Dole put together a bill calling for the spending of between $1.3 billion and $1.6 billion to fight illegal drug use but dropped the Senate Democrats' provision for a drug czar along with proposals of Republicans in both houses for the death penalty and modifying the exclusionary rule. While increasing the military's involvement in the interdiction of drug shipments, the bipartisan Senate approach did not authorize the soldiers and sailors to arrest civilians.[3]

So far, the responses of the two houses to the drug problem were similar, but voices were being heard in the Senate against hasty and precipitate action. Senator Lowell P. Weicker, Jr. (R-Conn.), was even able to teach a little constitutional lesson to his colleagues. It concerned the manner in which the anti-drug crusade would be financed. The Dole-Byrd bipartisan package called for the anti-drug campaign to be financed in part by a checkoff on taxpayers' IRS forms. Citizens would contribute a portion of their tax refund to fighting drugs by checking a box on the front of their form. Such a checkoff was estimated by Dole to be capable of yielding $500 million annually to fight drugs.

Weicker, who opposed what he saw as the punitive spirit of the bill, reminded his colleagues that one feature of the measure would be a violation of the Constitution. After all, the checkoff system was revenue-raising legislation, and such measures must originate in the House, not in the Senate. Only temporarily stymied, the sponsors merely changed the bill by adding the Senate version as an amendment to the bill already passed by the House. Such substitutions are common devices in Congress to get around problems.

But transforming a Senate bill into an amendment to a bill already passed by the House did not ensure its passage. For a number of senators, the bill was "constitutionally suspect." Senator Daniel J. Evans (R-Wash.) attacked the measure as a "sanctimonious election year stampede that will trample the Constitution." Pointing to the use of the military to arrest drug suspects, the death penalty, and the relaxation of the rules of evidence, Evans warned, "If we vote for legislation to win an election [the 1986 congressional elections were two months away] and trample the Constitution in the process, we have not served the country very well."[4]

It was not that the Senate regarded the problem as less urgent than did the House—moderate Florida Democrat Lawton Chiles vowed that the bill would not "die on the doorstep"—but rather that the distinctive roles and styles of the two houses were beginning to express themselves in the response of the Senate to the House.[5]

By mid-October, the sticking point in the negotiations between the two chambers was obvious. The House bill contained the death penalty and the Senate version did not. A bipartisan group of twenty-five senators—eleven Republicans and fourteen Democrats—sent their respective leaders messages saying that the inclusion of the House-passed death penalty provision would "make it extremely difficult if not impossible to complete action on the bill." Backing up the warning was the threat of "extended debate"—the dreaded filibuster—just a month before congressional elections.[6]

While House leaders were inclined to accept the Senate version without the death penalty, they were aware that sentiment among their colleagues for the provision was very strong, and probably irresistible. Speaker Tip O'Neill said, "I've never been for the death penalty, but there's no question the votes are there." Even the most intransigent foe of the death penalty on the House side, Representative Don Edwards of California, reluctantly agreed that it had the votes to pass his chamber. Edwards did note with relief that the new House version had dropped the modification of the exclusionary rule.

But it was the eagerness of House members for the death penalty and the certainty that a bill with such a provision would be filibustered to death in the waning days of the 99th Congress that posed the threat of adjournment with no action at all on a pressing problem.

In a move reminiscent of the 1962 House-Senate impasse over appropriations some House tacticians suggested adjourning and presenting the Senate with a take-it-or-leave-it situation: Accept the House drug bill with the death penalty provision or suffer the consequences of having no bill, because House members would have left so there would be no one around to bargain with.

This ploy turned out to be unnecessary. A Senate partnership between ultra-conservative Republican J. Strom Thurmond of South Carolina and liberal Democrat Joseph Biden of Delaware organized an informal conference in the Speaker's dining room of the Capitol (on the House side) and after three hours worked out a compromise. Funding was provided for the anti-drug effort, but absent from the bill were the death penalty, the provision to weaken the exclusionary law, and the requirement that the military be used to intercept and arrest drug smugglers.[7] President Reagan signed the bill on October 27, 1986.

If congressional action on anti-drug legislation had ended there, what might have been concluded about the differences between the House and Senate on policy for coping with illegal drugs?

First, it might have been said that the House was able to act swiftly to frame legislation. Members picked up quickly on public concern about drugs. The House was also writing into its bills in direct and undiluted form the rage and frustration of the citizens with the drug problems. It came through in the death penalty provision, in the willingness to modify the restrictions on illegally obtained evidence, and in the readiness to use troops to interdict drugs and to vest them with the power to arrest civilians.

About the Senate, it might have been said that there was clearly a sense that action was required, but a quarter of the membership, composed of both Democrats and Republicans, considered the House measures harsh, and even of dubious constitutionality. These senators were adamant that no death penalty provision be included, and vowed to use the filibuster if necessary to knock out the capital punishment clause. Indeed, on October 16, Republican senator Charles McCurdy Mathias of Maryland stood toe-to-toe in Robert Dole's office with the author of the House death penalty amendment, Pennsylvania Republican representative George W. Gekas, and told him that he was prepared to filibuster the death penalty issue until Christmas.[8]

An advocate of responsive government and law and order would have seen in the action of the House a promptness in conformity with the sentiments of the people but would have found the Senate's approach irresponsibly casual and unduly vulnerable to the views of an overly scrupulous minority.

An exponent of civil liberties, individual rights, and strict divisions between civil and military functions would have found the House hasty and precipitous, caring more for heeding the hysteria of the public than for cultivating individual rights and a proper role for the military. The same people would have applauded the Senate for its staunch defense of those constitutional principles and concluded that the institution was doing precisely what the framers of the Constitution had intended. So, if indeed anti-drug policy had ended there, it would have been a textbook case of a Senate with a wariness for hasty action and a solicitude for individual rights bringing to bear its procedural safeguards against a House inflamed by the passions of the moment.

The 1986 law, however, was not the final word on the policy to combat illegal drugs. Within two years, it became clear that new legislation was required. By the spring of 1988, the new House Speaker, Jim Wright of Texas, was lamenting, "The war on drugs is not being won. We've got to do more."[9]

Two years had passed in which the inadequacies of the 1986 legislation had become evident to members of Congress. Brutal gang wars were being waged in American cities over control of narcotics traffic, and violence by drug dealers against law enforcement officials had escalated. This time, however, the cry for swift, sure, and harsh punishment arose in the Senate.

It was another election year—this time a presidential campaign was under way and drugs were at the top of the voters' list of concerns. Just about the time that George Bush and Michael Dukakis had sewn up their parties' nominations, New York Republican Alfonse D'Amato rose in the Senate to vow, "It is about time we say to the Darth Vaders of the drug world that you will face the ultimate sanction." The Senate, which had two years before balked at a death penalty for drug-related murders, using threats of filibusters, swallowed the death penalty on a 65–29 vote.

What had changed? Had the Senate become more bloody-minded and retributive in the ensuing two years? Had it conceded that the House had been right all along? If the twenty-nine who voted against capital punishment cared enough, why did they not filibuster in 1988? For foes of the death penalty, was the Senate no longer a reliable bulwark against capital punishment, and, as such, a lesser institution? Should an advocate of execution for drug-related murders come to the conclusion that the Senate had finally come to its senses and gotten in line with the House and its sensitivity to the wishes of the people?

The change is best not seen in such stark terms. The events of 1988 did not constitute a triumph for the responsiveness of the House and a defeat for the deliberateness of the Senate.

It is important to recognize that it was not the intent of the framers of the Constitution for the Senate to thwart the will of the people, just to temper it. There was a less perfectly formed public consensus about what measures needed to be taken to cope with the illegal drug problem in 1986 than there was in 1988. But even the apparent consensus on the desirability of imposing the death penalty did not extend to such measures as the use of the armed forces to interdict supplies of drugs from abroad. The House continued to favor granting the armed services broad powers of arrest while the Senate remained disinclined to involve the military. This difference was exemplified in a House-passed provision of May 1988 to direct the Department of Defense to "substantially" reduce drug smuggling within forty-five days. Senate conferees on the bill argued successfully for narrowing the scope and, finally, for eliminating involvement by the armed forces, while leaving open the possibility of a role for the National Guard in a support capacity.[10]

As the discussions extended through the summer and fall of 1988, they took characteristic forms depending on whether they were taking place in the House or Senate. Senate discussions aimed for a bipartisan bill and daily discussion proceeded between staff members of Republican leader Dole and Democratic leader Byrd. In the House, however, leaders of the Democratic majority specifically rejected a bipartisan approach in favor of one that was the product of twelve separate committees in which provisions would be added or deleted, in most instances, by party-line votes.[11]

The Senate discussions were not without their partisan side and in a manner characteristic of that chamber, the introduction of nongermane amendments threatened to derail the bill. These were a series of anti-pornography amendments by Republicans that would have given the federal government sweeping powers to seize the assets of those distributing any material deemed obscene by a state court. Opponents claimed that this would have enabled the government to put a convenience store out of business for selling copies of *Playboy* that a local court had ruled obscene.[12]

The mischievous partisan purpose of these amendments was to force Democratic senators a few weeks before elections to go on record on an anti-pornography vote of dubious constitutionality. The most drastic Senate provision was actually adopted but later eliminated in conference.

The partisanship on the Senate side, however, was more restrained by what seemed to be the general objective of producing a bill that the entire membership could stand behind, rather than to come up with a legislation on which the only fingerprints belonged to the majority. With the Senate as a whole standing behind the bill, there was a sense among senators that what they had come up with was a superior bill to the one in the House because all sides had been heard and their views accommodated. It was legislation more nearly in line with the common good because it was the product of an undertaking in a legislative body where consensus is prized over efficiency, over the clarity of a partisan message, and even over the need to satisfy an electorate that demanded drastic action even if that action turned out to be wrongheaded.

As Mansbridge recognized in her observations of groups in which direct and personal contact are the rule, "in spite of the costs in time, repetition, [and] occasional lack of clarity, requiring consensus has significant advantages whenever interests can be reconciled. It directs members' attention and communication on dissidents, trying to draw them into the group."[13]

Republicans and Democrats in the Senate were divided over the severity of punishment for drug users and the balance that needed to be struck between attacking the supply side (interdiction of drug shipments entering the country) and attacking the demand side (user penalties and addict rehabilitation programs). Senate Democrats believed that Republican emphasis on the supply side was the pursuit of a policy that had shown poor results. Senate Republicans were said to be contemptuous of an approach that emphasized cutting the demand. But what characterized the Senate as a whole was that all sides could live with a bill that provided resources for both approaches.[14]

While neither side in the Senate was won over to the other's arguments, the Senate environment provided a setting for a learning to take place and for that learning to form the basis of legislation that is more oriented to the common good because it is more a product of a common undertaking. Such an environment "encourages people to listen carefully to both the emotional tone and intellectual content of what others say. It helps bring out information, forges commitment, discourages factions, and creates the morale-building sense that 'we are all in this together.' "[15]

But is this kind of solidarity-building exercise among senators a phenomenon that is useful only for the Senate as an institution? What were the American people, perplexed by the plague of drugs and the violence it bred, getting out of this? Was the public policy that would ultimately emerge be better for the nation as a whole because of the interplay of these two very different institutional styles?

Without question, most Americans would have preferred striking out at the drug dealers with the harshest and most direct penalties and would not have agonized too much about the arcane rules of evidence or the proper use of the military. They were hurting and the House responded to that affliction in a timely manner that was in keeping with the intensity of public feeling.

The House was harkening to a public outcry and formulating a strong dose of sanctions to be applied to the drug trade. Citizens could reassure themselves that something was being done in a timely and forceful fashion.

But then it fell to the Senate to ensure that it was the *right* thing that was being done. Or, at least, that the amount of wrong was kept within bounds and that the result of congressional action was not only good politics but good policy.

As recently as a month before final passage, the House version of the bill had come under fire from some of its own members concerned about the adverse effects of some provisions on individual rights. Representative William J. Hughes, a New Jersey Democrat and chairman of the Criminal Law Subcommittee of the House Judiciary Committee, condemned segments of the bill as being of "dubious constitutionality."[16]

But by the time the conference was finished with the bill, a number of Senate provisions had softened the House measure to the point where a staff member to a liberal senator who had seen the House bill as a threat to civil liberties could conclude, "We have done a good thing; this is now a worthwhile bill."[17]

The Senate had managed to narrow the circumstances in which capital punishment could be applied in drug-related killings. The Senate conferees also succeeded in deleting from the bill a House amendment that would have weakened the exclusionary rule and allowed the introduction in criminal cases of evidence seized in warrantless searches in which police officers had had a "good faith" belief that they were acting legally. In the case of a provision to deny certain federal benefits, such as public housing, to those convicted of drug offenses, there was a considerable difference between the House and Senate versions. The House bill would have denied these benefits to those found guilty of drug-related crimes. The Senate version that ultimately prevailed gave judges discretion as to whether such penalties could be imposed.

Finally, the Senate modified considerably a House-passed amendment that would have allowed fines of up to $10,000 to be imposed on people found possessing small quantities of drugs for personal use. What was novel about this provision and alarming to civil libertarians was that the Justice Department could have directed that such people be tried in a civil hearing rather than stand trial in a regular criminal court. Conducted by a hearing examiner rather than a judge, the normal rules of evidence that protect criminal defendants would be replaced by a system in which it would be far easier to get a conviction. The Senate changed this to allow defendants to insist on a criminal trial with the greater safeguards for the accused.

On the whole, then, the hand of law enforcement officials was strengthened against the illegal drug traffic without doing violence to the Constitution. By acting in their characteristic adversary and unitary ways, the House and Senate were balancing off responsiveness with responsibility.

What the example of the drug bills shows is that not only are the House and Senate not converging, but they *should not* converge.

A House that functioned as a large Senate and a Senate that was a House in miniature would not serve well the balance between the two expressions of democracy: the adversary form that is a safeguard against the alienation that can afflict citizens in a mass society, and reassures them that their interests are being looked after, and the unitary form that reminds them that they are part of something greater and that there is an overall good that needs tending to so as to allow the survival of the larger political community.

NOTES

1. Edward Walsh, "It Comes Down to One Young Man Not Dying in Vain," *Washington Post,* National Weekly Edition, September 29–October 5, 1986.
2. Ibid.
3. Julie Rovner, "Senate Takes Up Compromise Anti-Drug Bill," *Congressional Quarterly Weekly Report,* September 27, 1986, p. 2266.
4. Ibid.
5. Julie Rovner, "Massive Anti-Drug Measure Ready for Reagan's Signature," *Congressional Quarterly Weekly Report,* October 25, 1986, p. 2699.
6. Julie Rovner, "Death Penalty Filibuster Threat Snags Anti-Drug Bill in Senate," *Congressional Quarterly Weekly Report,* October 11, 1986, p. 2574.
7. Rovner, "Massive Anti-Drug Measure Ready," p. 2699.
8. Julie Rovner, "With Death Penalty Removed, Anti-Drug Measure Cleared," *Congressional Quarterly Weekly Report,* October 18, 1986, p. 2594.
9. Irwin Molotsky, "House Leaders Call for Swift Passage of a Bill to Fight Illegal Drugs," *New York Times,* May 10, 1988.
10. Michael Isikoff, "Launching Nuclear Bombs in a Guerilla War," *Washington Post,* National Weekly Edition, August 1–7, 1988, p. 33.
11. Charles Mohr, "Proposed Drug Bill Tests the Art of Compromise," *New York Times,* Tuesday, August 2, 1988.
12. Tom Kenworthy and Helen Dewar, "Conferees Agree on Drug Bill," *Washington Post,* Friday, October 21, 1988.
13. Jane J. Mansbridge, *Beyond Adversary Democracy* (Chicago: University of Chicago Press, 1983), p. 165.
14. Mohr, "Proposed Drug Bill Tests the Art."
15. Mansbridge, op. cit., p. 165.
16. Charles Mohr, "Negotiators for House and Senate in a Virtual Accord on Drug Bill," *New York Times,* Friday, October 21, 1988.
17. Irwin Molotsky, "With End of the Session in Sight, Congress Votes to Curb Lobbying," *New York Times,* Saturday, October 22, 1988.

Index

231